The Christian Brethren as the Nineties Began

Peter Brierley
Graham Brown
Boyd Myers
Harold Rowdon
Neil Summerton

Published for
PARTNERSHIP
in association with MARC Europe
by
THE PATERNOSTER PRESS
Carlisle, UK

British Library Cataloguing in Publication Data

Brierley, Peter
   Christian Brethren as the Nineties Began
   I. Title II. Rowdon, Harold H.
   289.9
   ISBN 0–900128–09–7

*Typeset in Great Britain by Photoprint, 9–11 Alexandra Lane,
Torquay, published for Partnership by The Paternoster Press,
P.O. Box 300, Carlisle, Cumbria, CA3 0QS, U.K., and
printed by BPCC Periodicals Ltd., Exeter, Devon.*

Contents

Contents

Introduction

Evangelical Christianity across the world comprises a wide variety of different groups. Some are full-blown denominations with centralised structures; others are no more than loose associations or movements. Some begin as para-church societies or evangelistic associations, but with success in church-planting evolve into denominations though they may have set out to avoid doing so.

Generally today each of these denominations and groups does not think of itself as the exclusive bearer of Christian truth even on the characteristic features which distinguish them from other Evangelical groups: increasingly they wish to emphasize the unity which they share in Christ with other Biblically-based Christians. Nevertheless most of these groups retain a sense of individual identity, and understand that their distinctive origins and experiences to some extent condition current possibilities for change and growth. So it is often worthwhile for them to discuss matters of special interest only to themselves. This is true even of comparatively young groups: it is the more so with those which already have a long and distinctive history.

To help the process, they frequently find it useful to try to assess their current state objectively, including by means of statistical measurement. Perhaps because Christian (Open) Brethren leaders have frequently been involved in the secular business world which takes such measurement for granted, some have shown a perhaps surprising readiness to measure the progress of their movement. In 1966 a small survey was undertaken by the then recently founded Christian Brethren Research Fellowship (CBRF).[1] This was followed up twelve years later by a more substantial and methodologically-advanced survey.[2] Both studies provided an interesting snapshot of the state and characteristics of the churches which were surveyed, and permitted some conclusions to be drawn about what God was then doing through the network of churches as a whole.

In 1988 Partnership (as the CBRF is now known) decided that it would be well worth conducting a further study. The approach was somewhat different—focussing on factual questions and omitting the attitudinal questions of 1978 which had been difficult to interpret, especially as they were particularly dependent on the views of the particular individual completing the questionnaire. Nevertheless, the series of three surveys over two decades does enable some conclusions to be drawn about the evolution of the responding churches, and possibly of the Christian Brethren movement as a whole in the British Isles, over that period. A longer perspective still is given by the study of Brethren growth over the period 1850–1960 in Appendix 1.

Separately, in October 1989, the English Church Census surveyed church-attendance and characteristics in all Christian congregations in England, including Brethren congregations of all varieties, Open and Exclusive. The response to that survey by congregations defining themselves as Open Brethren provides both additional infor-

---

1 Graham D Brown, 'How can we improve our evangelism?—Deductions from a survey of assemblies', *The Journal of the Christian Brethren Research Fellowship*, No. 21, May 1971, pp. 44–57. The survey was 'primarily to discover the place of evangelism in the church's aims, its evangelistic endeavours, their results and areas of success or otherwise.' 75 congregations were surveyed, mainly by means of a questionnaire completed by interview. The congregations were selected so as 'to cover all sizes and types of "open" assembly in each part of England and Wales, rural as well as urban.'
2 Graham Brown and Brian Mills, *'The Brethren' today: a factual survey*, Exeter: The Paternoster Press and the Christian Brethren Research Fellowship, 1980. The survey was again conducted by questionnaire completed by interview. Questionnaires were completed in respect of 249 congregations 'representing most geographical areas of England and Wales (and a few churches from Scotland), and different shades of opinion (as illustrated by the attitudinal questions) . . .' 70 of these congregations were among the 75 congregations surveyed in 1966.

mation and a very valuable cross-check on the response to the 1988 survey. The results are set out in chapter 8.

The English Church Census is a further invaluable contribution to the life of the church as a whole in this country through the statistical analysis by Peter Brierley, the European Director of MARC Europe. His work appears in successive editions of the *UK Christian Handbook* and it permits comparison on some key variables between the Christian Brethren and similar denominational groupings. These comparisons are included in chapter 9. They can give a further dimension to the strategic thinking required if Christian Brethren congregations are to receive blessing from the Lord in renewed growth in the coming decade. For our purpose is not simply antiquarian: we believe that they can give us the equivalent of a navigational fix as we map out the future course to which God is calling us as churches, and can help us to draw lessons which will be of value in the next stages of the voyage.[3]

It is the nature of such studies that they are the work of many hands. The 1988 survey was mainly the work of Graham Brown, with assistance from John Boyes and Neil Summerton in devising the questionnaire. The analysis of data and the production of tables and diagrams has been exclusively the work of Graham Brown. We are enormously indebted to Peter Brierley and Boyd Myers on his staff not only for chapter 8 on the Christian Brethren response to the English Church Census, but also for preparing successive drafts of the introduction and chapters 2–7: had Peter Brierley not volunteered to do this, it is doubtful if in the circumstances the survey results could have been published. Neil Summerton and Graham Brown have read these drafts and must be regarded as responsible for any errors of interpretation. Any blame for chapter 9 and appendix 1 lies exclusively with Neil Summerton. Appendix 4 was prepared by Harold Rowdon.

---

3 The gift of administration in 1 Corinthians 12:28 is literally that of the steersman, and all groups of Christian congregations need strategic vision if they are to flourish.

Our special thanks must of course go to all who completed the postal questionnaire. Without their work these studies would not have been possible, and we are grateful for their interest. We hope that this report will be some reward.

Our collective prayer is that this volume will stimulate congregational leaders, and those responsible for the various trusts and associations which seek to support those congregations, in the directions which are necessary if the movement is to regain spiritual vitality within Evangelical Christianity as a whole in the British Isles.

1

The Survey of 1988:
Methods and Significance

The Partnership survey of 1988 was conducted purely by way of a postal questionnaire. A copy of the questionnaire is reproduced at Appendix 2. We relied wholly on the willingness of individuals to complete and return it. Only one set of questionnaires was sent out and no other reminders were issued. To economise effort, there were, quite unlike the surveys of 1966 and 1978, no attempts to make personal contact with congregations to give assistance in the completion of the questionnaire.

Copies were sent to all churches in the British Isles which were included in a list based on the assembly address list published in 1983.[1] 308 responses were sent back, a response rate of about 20%. This was disappointingly low and it is interesting that the completely separate, externally-conducted English Church Census achieved a response rate from Christian Brethren churches of 38% (using the 1983 list as the survey frame updated with other information and

---

1 *Christian Brethren Assemblies round the World*, Glasgow: Pickering and Inglis, 1983.

a postal method—but with two postal reminders).[2] This suggests a high degree of unwillingness, or inability for structural reasons, in Christian Brethren assemblies to participate in statistical studies. It may also say something about the way in which the bulk of Christian Brethren assemblies today see themselves in relation to an organisation like Partnership,[3] and to a mainstream inter-denominational body like MARC Europe and the English Church Census.[4]

The low rate of response, and the absolute size of the resulting sample, may raise questions, as it did in respect of the 1978 survey, about the accuracy and relevance of the results.

It is true that we should be cautious about interpreting the results. The responding churches were self-selecting and cannot with certainty be assumed to be representative of Christian Brethren churches as a body. But a glance at the returned questionnaires would convince anyone familiar with the assemblies that the 308 responses were from a very wide range of churches. So the responses should not simply be dismissed as not giving a reliable indication of the

---

2 249 congregations responded to the 1978 survey, 308 to the 1988 survey, and 357 to the English Church Census in 1989. In greater detail the response was as follows:

Those responding in 1978 only	116
Those responding in 1978 and 1988 only	60
Those responding in 1978 and 1989 only	36
Those responding in 1978, 1988, and 1989	37
Those responding in 1988 only	142
Those responding in 1988 and 1989 only	69
Those responding in 1989 only	215
Total	675

Therefore something like half of Brethren congregations have been willing to respond to at least one survey in the last 15 years, and a third of those responded only to an externally-mounted survey.

3 One or two letters were received protesting against the principle of such a statistical survey.

4 It is interesting that the interdenominational body achieved nearly twice the response rate achieved by the overtly Brethren body.

5 The term 'assembly' is less frequently used than it used to be, particularly in the more progressive churches which would now more readily (and prefer to) identify themselves by the term 'church' than they did two generations ago. However, 'assemblies' is a convenient term to describe in short compass 'Christian Brethren churches/congregations', and it is extensively used in that sense in this volume.

character of the assemblies[5] as a body. And insofar as the 308 responses can be taken as representative, they are more than enough to give statistically significant (ie, reliable) results—many sociological studies of much larger populations depend on samples which are very much smaller and are accepted as being statistically valid.

It can in any case be said with certainty that the 308 responses are a 100% sample of those 308 congregations and that the results can accordingly be taken as reliably characterising that considerable number of congregations. And insofar as there were any bias in the responses towards the more progressive assemblies, the survey could be regarded as being more reliable as an inquiry into that type of assembly.

The inevitable uncertainties notwithstanding, our view is that it would be unwise simply to dismiss the data reported in this volume, or the implications that they have.

2

Size and Trends from the 1988 Survey

The overall picture

How many assemblies of Christian (Open) Brethren are there altogether in the United Kingdom, and what is the probable total membership of these assemblies? The 1983 address list already cited gave their number as 1,555, and the new lists prepared by Christian Year Publications give the numbers as 1,404 in 1990 and 1,380 in 1991.[1] Drawing on information about the average size of assembly (see below) and using linear extrapolation, the 1992/93 Edition of the *UK Christian Handbook* puts the total membership of these congregations at 66,000 in 1985 and 63,200 in 1990. More detailed figures for 1990 are:

Table 1: Number of assemblies and their membership

Open Brethren	1985 UK	1990 UK	1990 England	1990 Wales	1990 Scotland	1990 N. Ireland
Assemblies	1,560	1,537	977	102	277	181
Members	66,000	63,200	41,100	4,700	11,200	6,200

The 1992/93 Edition also, for the first time, gives basic information on other types of Brethren assembly. It is worth

---

1 *The Assemblies Address Book 1990* and *idem 1991*, Bristol: Christian Year Publications. Roy Hill has, if only for the statisticians, performed a very useful service in taking up the publication of this series of address lists.

noting here that it suggests that in 1990 there were 390 Plymouth Brethren No. 4 ('Taylorite') assemblies with 12,018 members, and altogether 81 assemblies of the remaining types, with 2,175 members.[2] So if the *Handbook* is correct, Christian (Open) Brethren assemblies account for 77% of Brethren assemblies of all types in the United Kingdom and 82% of their members—indicating that on average other types of assembly are slightly smaller than the average Open assembly.[3]

Size of assemblies

The first question in the questionnaire asked about the size of the responding congregation, defining this either as the number in fellowship/membership or the number of Christians who regularly attended at the time of the response.[4] Which of the alternatives used by the respondent was not indicated and some ambiguity could therefore arise, since membership numbers can exceed regular attendance or *vice versa*, and indeed the definition of 'regular' attendance can vary from one congregation to another. The results are given below and show an average assembly size of 52, compared with a national average of 82 for all Christian congregations (excluding Roman Catholic congregations —which are large in size as a result of a different church-planting strategy, and distort the overall figure). Brethren congregations therefore tend to be smaller than average, perhaps reflecting attitudes towards the nature of church

---

2 It is interesting that 105 No. 4 congregations responded to the English Church Census in 1989, a response rate of 35%, and that the Census suggested that they had been growing modestly in numbers between 1979 and 1989.
3 Though over the years there has been some cross-fertilisation of membership, and theological and ecclesiological ideas, between the Exclusive and Open wings of the Brethren movement, readers unfamiliar with the history should note that the two wings have developed separately since the mid-nineteenth century. No. 4 churches now have a very different character from Open Brethren churches.
4 Practice varies between Brethren congregations: some keep lists of believers regarded as having committed themselves to membership of the particular fellowship; in others, 'membership' is more informal, being those believers who attend on a regular basis.

fellowship, and the structure and operation of ministry in the assemblies.[5]

Table 2: Size of assembly

Partnership Survey 1988		English Church Census 1989		
No. of members or regular attenders	Percentage %	No of attenders	Percentage %	(1988 Partnership Survey %)
0– 9	4	1– 25	31	(27)
10–19	14			
20–29	18	26– 50	27	(30)
30–39	11	51– 75	17	(19)
40–49	10			
50–59	11	76–100	13	(15)
60–79	11	101 or over	12	(9)
80–99	12			
100 or over	9			

The cumulated figures in Table 2 are plotted in Figure 1. Table 2 compares the similar data in the Brethren response to the English Church Census. The Census used different size-bands from the 1988 survey; even so, the agreement between the two is fairly close, bearing in mind that slightly more large churches responded in the Census.

Figure 2 compares the sizes of assemblies in 1988 with that of the survey carried out in 1978. Although the proportion of churches with over 100 members had fallen from 15% in 1978 to 9% in 1988, the overall differences between the two surveys are not great. Indeed, the average mean in 1978 was 52 identical to that in 1988 thus showing stability over this ten year period.

Figure 3 gives an indication of the size of assemblies across the United Kingdom in 1988, based on the data in Table 3.

_____

5 Chapter 8 gives a more detailed analysis of average size of congregation compared with those of other denominations.

What is the size of your church? 1988

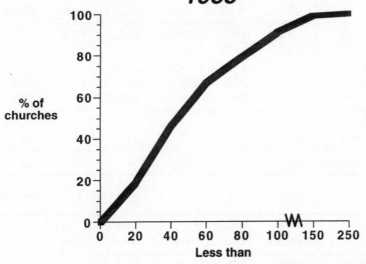

Source: 1988 Survey of Brethren Churches

Figure 1: Size of Assemblies 1988

What is the size of your church? 1978 v 1988

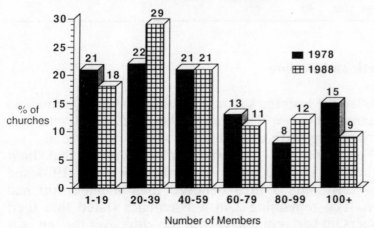

Source: 1978/1988 Surveys of Brethren Churches

Figure 2: Size of Assemblies 1978 and 1988

Table 3: Size of assemblies 1988 by region

Size	North-East	North-West	York-shire	Mid-lands	East Anglia	South East
0–19	30%	18%	14%	14%	17%	13%
20–29	10%	18%	14%	23%	21%	13%
30–49	10%	14%	14%	29%	21%	33%
50–79	30%	21%	58%	14%	12%	26%
80 or over	20%	29%	0%	20%	29%	15%
Total (=100%)	10	28	7	35	24	39
Average size	51	57	48	50	55	51

Size	London	South West	Wales	Scot-land	N. Ire-land	UK
0–19	23%	22%	10%	18%	15%	18%
20–29	28%	17%	32%	11%	8%	18%
30–49	13%	28%	32%	18%	0%	21%
50–79	18%	19%	26%	27%	23%	23%
80 or over	18%	14%	0%	26%	54%	20%
Total (=100%)	39	36	19	55	13	305
Average size	46	45	39	58	78	52

Growth and Decline

Although the average size of a Brethren assembly remained the same between 1978 and 1988, individual churches experienced growth or decline, as shown in Figure 4.

Four Brethren assemblies in 9 believed that their membership had declined in numbers between 1978 and 1988 whilst only 3 in 9 believed their membership had grown. The remaining 2 in 9 assemblies stated that their membership had remained about the same over the ten year period. Although there were fewer growing churches than declining churches over this period overall numbers gained

Size of Assemblies by Region 1988

Figure 3: Size of Assemblies by region 1988

Has the church grown in the past 10 years?

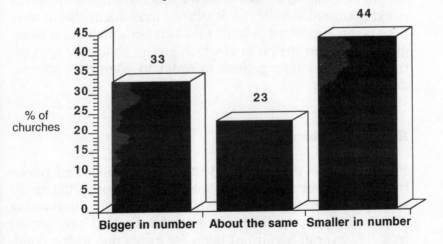

Figure 4: Assembly change 1978–1988

matched overall numbers lost as the unchanged average mean size of an assembly between 1978 and 1988 shows.

Nearly 2 in 5 assemblies believed they had either greatly increased (10%) or slightly increased (29%) in numbers between 1983 and 1988 (an improvement on the period 1978–1988). However, 4 in 9 assemblies had either slightly decreased (36%) or greatly decreased (8%) in numbers over the same period (no improvement on the period 1978–1988). The remaining 16% of assemblies experienced no change in overall numbers.

Figure 5 opposite shows that Brethren assemblies which attracted relatively large congregations also tended to be the growing churches whilst Brethren churches which attracted small congregations also tended to be the declining churches over the five year period. (This is reinforced by Figure 7). Indeed 2 in 4 of the largest 100 assemblies had experienced growth between 1983 and 1988 in contrast to only 1 in 4 of the smallest 100 assemblies, whilst nearly 6 in 10 of the smallest 100 assemblies had experienced decline in contrast to nearly 3 in 10 of the largest 100 assemblies.

This trend was also found by the English Church Census in 1989 carried out by MARC Europe. If this trend continues the future viability of many of these smallest assemblies will be at risk. Given common attitudes towards congregational size in the Brethren movement, there may here be an important pointer for churches which are seeking growth, and for the point at which groups should be split off from existing congregations in order to plant new congregations.

Reasons for change

Figure 6 shows that overall Brethren assemblies had grown by 2.6% between 1986 and 1988. This was solely the result of growth through conversions of both adults and young people. Indeed, the Brethren assemblies would have grown by 4.3% overall had it not been for losses due to the death of elderly members and other members leaving the assembly for a variety of reasons.

Has the church grown or declined in the last five years?

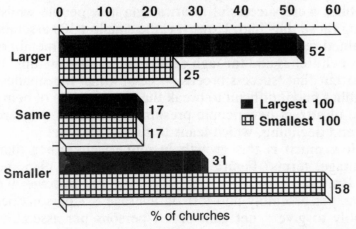

Figure 5: Assembly change 1983–1988 for the largest 100 and smallest 100 assemblies

Has the church grown or declined in the last two years?

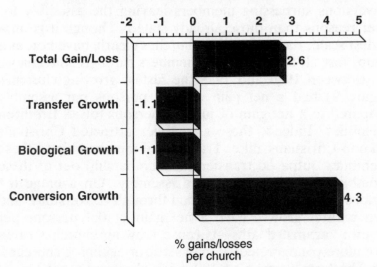

Figure 6: Assembly change 1986–1988 by reason for change

The largest 100 assemblies experienced an average overall growth of 5.5% between 1986 and 1988. In contrast the smallest 100 assemblies experienced a decline of 3% over the same period. Figure 7 shows that the largest 100 assemblies were successful in attracting new people whilst keeping those they had. However, the smallest 100 assemblies gained relatively few new people whilst losing members to other churches and through deaths in their fellowships. It is apparent that 'success breeds success' whilst the smallest assemblies find it difficult to break the vicious circle of being unable to attract new people presumably because they are small and declining, which leads to further decline.

How much is this growth in numerical, rather than percentage, terms? Figure 8 shows that between 1986 and 1988 Brethren assemblies both gained on average 9.6 persons per assembly and lost on average 8.2 persons per assembly to give a net gain of 1.4 persons per assembly. There was a net loss of 0.5 persons per assembly due to a transfer of membership to other denominations and also a net loss of 0.6 persons through deaths outstripping natural growth (this is due to the large proportion of elderly in many assemblies, as will be seen in the Census section). However, there was a net gain of 2.1 persons per church through conversions surpassing members leaving the assembly for other reasons than those already stated. Though it is on a modest scale, the responding churches clearly have not, as a group, lost all ability to add members through conversion.

Between 1986 and 1988 the fastest growing churches (Figure 9) had a net gain of 10.2 persons per assembly compared to a net gain of just 1.4 persons for all Brethren assemblies. Indeed, these assemblies attracted Christians and non-Christians alike. Transfers of membership to these assemblies outpaced transfers of membership out of these assemblies by 3.7 persons per assembly. On average 6.4 persons per assembly were added through conversions, and even natural growth gave a net gain of 0.4 persons per assembly against deaths—because growing churches often have more younger people than static or declining churches.

The fastest declining 100 assemblies saw a net loss of 8.5 persons per assembly between 1986 and 1988, a very

Has the church grown or declined in the last two years?
Largest 100 v Smallest 100

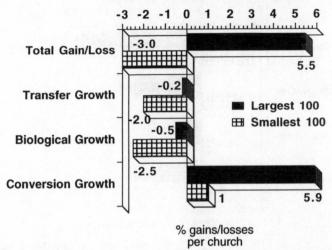

% gains/losses
per church

Source: 1988 Survey of Brethren Churches

Figure 7: Assembly change 1986–1988 by reason and size of church

What is the growth or decline in the last two years?
All churches

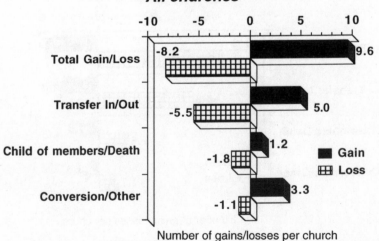

Number of gains/losses per church

Source: 1988 Survey of Brethren Churches

Figure 8: Assembly change 1986–1988 by numbers gained or lost

What is the growth or decline in the last two years?
Fastest Growing 100 churches

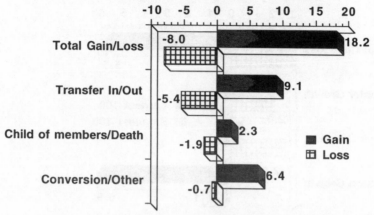

Number of gains/losses per church

Source: 1988 Survey of Brethren Churches

Figure 9: Assembly change 1986–1988 by numbers gained or lost for the 100 fastest growing assemblies

What is the growth or decline in the last two years?
Fastest Declining 100 churches

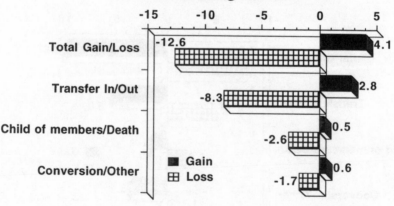

Number of gains/losses per church

Source: 1988 Survey of Brethren Churches

Figure 10: Assembly change 1986–1988 by numbers gained or lost for the 100 fastest declining churches

disturbing picture. Figure 10 shows that these assemblies saw few conversions, deaths outstripping natural growth by 2.1 persons per assembly, perhaps indicating that few families and young people are to be found in these fellowships. Indeed, transfers of membership out of these assemblies surpassed transfers of membership into these assemblies by 5.5 persons per assembly. The future for many of these assemblies is very bleak if such rapid decline continues. The sobering calculation is that, with an average loss of 8.5 persons per two years, most of these churches will have closed by 1998 unless the trend is altered.

Summary

Since the last survey in 1978, numbers have generally remained stable in the 308 responding churches. However a substantial minority (44%) of these assemblies had experienced decline between 1978 and 1988 and had it not been for vigorous growth in other assemblies the picture would be more worrying.

While the largest Brethren churches had as a group seen a growth in numbers, the smallest assemblies saw decline. If the decline, which pre-dates 1978 in many cases, continues the future for many of these smallest assemblies is bleak as members, finance, leadership and other resources dry up. Perhaps the larger growing Brethren assemblies could provide practical support for small struggling assemblies which are often to be found in the needy inner city and village environments.

3

Conversions and Baptisms

How far was the growth of responding churches attributable to conversion?

Conversions in the last two years

A large majority of Brethren asemblies (71%) saw at least one conversion between 1986 and 1988. Although 3 in 10 assemblies had no conversions during this period, 1 in 5 of all assemblies saw 10 or more conversions. The remaining 1 in 2 assemblies saw between 1 and 9 conversions. The overall average number of conversions per Brethren assembly between 1986 and 1988 was four. These figures are illustrated in Figure 11.

The proportion of Brethren assemblies who had no conversions over a two year period rose from 23% in 1978 to 29% in 1988. Although it could be argued that this is not a dramatic rise, it does have serious implications for the Brethren movement if the trend continues. Church growth could quickly be replaced with overall decline. The comparison with 1978 is given in Figure 12 opposite (where the number converted are grouped slightly differently to Figure 11 to allow exact comparisons).

The majority of churches are experiencing less conversions than in 1978—though a slightly larger proportion of churches have seen 10 or more conversions than in 1978—which tends to imply that the bigger churches are even more active and the smaller churches less active.

In your church how many people were converted in the past two years?

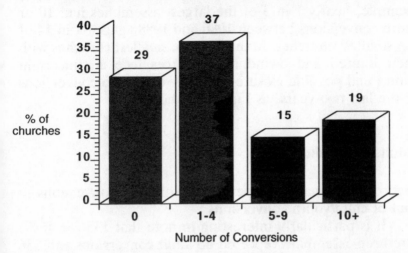

Source: 1988 Survey of Brethren Churches

Figure 11: Conversions per assembly 1986–1988

How many were converted in the last two years?
1978 v 1988

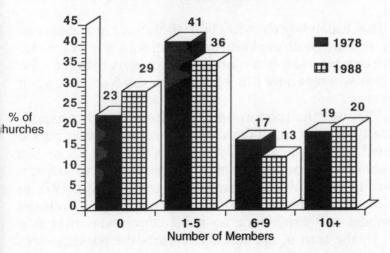

Source: 1978/1988 Surveys of Brethren Churches

Figure 12: Conversions per assembly 1978–1988

This conclusion is reinforced when the success of the largest churches in winning converts is contrasted with that of the smallest churches over the last two years. For example, nearly 1 in 3 of the largest assemblies had 10 or more conversions between 1986 and 1988 against 1 in 14 of the smallest churches. Many of these smallest churches with their limited and dwindling resources face an uncertain future and possible closure—half have seen no conversions in the last two years, as Figure 13 shows.

Adults and Children

Figure 14 compares the percentage of adult conversions to that of child/youth conversions.

It is particularly interesting to note that 135 (or 45%) Brethren assemblies reported no adult conversions and 136 (or 46%) assemblies reported no youth conversions between 1986 and 1988 whereas only 89 assemblies said they had no conversions at all during this period. This shows that 1 in 6 assemblies had youth conversions only during this period and 1 in 7 assemblies had adult conversions only with just 2 in 5 assemblies having both adult and youth conversions.

The responding churches as a whole were more successful in winning youth converts than adult converts. A quarter of all assemblies saw 5 or more youth converts between 1986 and 1988 whereas only 1 in 9 assemblies saw 5 or more adult converts.

Although the proportion of Brethren churches experiencing 10 or more adult conversions over a two year period doubled between 1978 and 1988, it was still only 4% or 1 in 25 assemblies. More disturbingly the proportion of assemblies seeing no adult conversions rose from 40% in 1978 to 45% in 1988; if this trend continues a majority of Brethren assemblies will experience no adult conversions over two years by the turn of the century. Clearly the consequences could be serious for the future of these churches unless decisive steps are taken to reverse this situation (Figure 15).

In your church how many people were converted in the last two years?
Largest 100 v Smallest 100

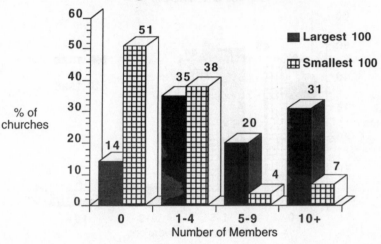

Source: 1988 Survey of Brethren Churches

Figure 13: Conversions per assembly 1986–1988 by size of assembly

In your church how many people were converted in the last two years?
Adults v Children

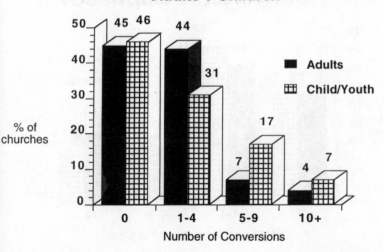

Source: 1988 Survey of Brethren Churches

Figure 14: Adult and child conversions per assembly 1986–1988

In your church how many adults were converted in the last two years?
1978 v 1988

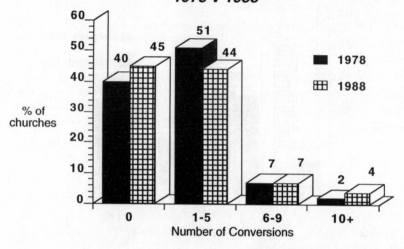

Source: 1978/1988 Surveys of Brethren Churches

Figure 15: Adult conversions per assembly 1978–1988

In your church, in the last two years how many people were Converted v Baptised?

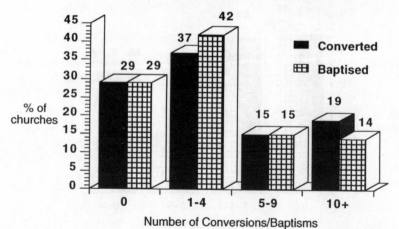

Source: 1988 Survey of Brethren Churches

Figure 16: Conversions and Baptisms per assembly 1986–1988

Baptisms

Not surprisingly, the proportion of Brethren assemblies who had no baptisms between 1986 and 1988 matched the proportion of assemblies who had no conversions. The proportion of assemblies who experienced 10 or more baptisms between 1986 and 1988 was slightly lower than the proportion of asemblies who gained 10 or more converts, indicating that not all converts follow through to baptism at least within the first two years. This may reflect the Brethren practice of not baptising converts immediately so that some may fall away before baptism takes place. This is illustrated in Figure 16.

The proportion of Brethren assemblies having 6 or more baptisms over a two year period declined from 35% in 1978 to 28% in 1988 while the proportion of Brethren assemblies having no baptisms rose from 26% in 1978 to 29% in 1988 as can be seen from Figure 17. There has been a slight overall decline in the number of baptisms between 1978 and 1988 reflecting a slight drop in the number of conversions.

It has already been noted that the smallest churches as a group experienced far fewer conversions between 1986 and 1988 than the largest churches. It is therefore not surprising to find that they also experienced far fewer baptisms as a group. More than half of the smallest assemblies had no baptisms between 1986 and 1988 compared to only 1 in 10 of the largest assemblies (Figure 18). In contrast, more than half of the largest assemblies saw 5 or more baptisms over the two year period compared to only 1 in 25 of the smallest assemblies.

Summary

The proportion of Brethren assemblies who had no conversions over a two year period rose from 23% in 1978 to 29% in 1988. This trend is a cause for concern particularly as many of these assemblies will already be among the smallest

How many were baptised in the last two years?
1978 v 1988

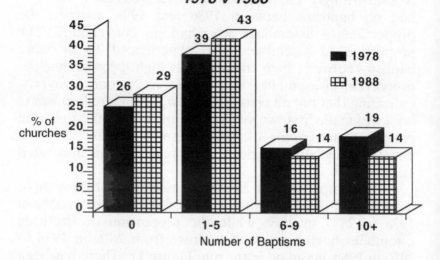

Source:1978/1988 Surveys of Brethren Churches

Figure 17: Baptisms per assembly over previous two years 1978–1988

In your church how many people were baptised in the last two years?
Largest 100 v Smallest 100

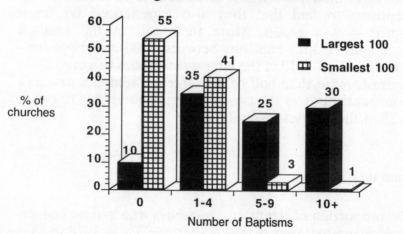

Source:1978/1988 Surveys of Brethren Churches

Figure 18: Baptisms per assembly 1986–1988 by size of assembly

in the Brethren movement. Eventual closure is facing many of these smallest assemblies.

Brethren assemblies as a whole tended to be more successful in winning youth converts than adult converts; only 1 in 9 assemblies saw 5 or more adult conversions compared to 1 in 4 assemblies who saw 5 or more youth conversions. This broad trend is similar to many other non-Brethren churches in Britain today. Like other churches they need to find ways of penetrating other age-groups with the Gospel. As might also be expected, assemblies who had a high number of conversions tended also to have a high number of baptisms.

4

Activities and Services

Main Activities

The questionnaire asked what were the main activities and services of this congregation.

More than 3 in 4 Brethren assemblies hold a Breaking of the Bread service, a Prayer Meeting, a Bible teaching activity, a Sunday School and a Gospel Meeting. A majority of Brethren assemblies also hold a Women's Meeting, a Family Service, a Bible Class and a Young People's fellowship.

Figure 20 compares the main services and activities of Brethren assemblies in 1988 with that of 1978. Over the ten year period, there were some significant changes with the Gospel Meeting moving from the second most frequently held meeting (96%) in 1978 to the fifth most frequently held in 1988 (77%). This is probably because this service had been replaced in some assemblies with a Family Service (64% of assemblies in 1988 compared to 43% in 1978) as new ways were sought to attract non-Christians and Christians alike to church. ('The Brethren Today' survey (1978) found that 75% of assemblies which held a Family Service in 1978 rated it more successful than a Gospel Meeting). However, the Gospel Meeting was still held by 3 in 4 assemblies in 1988 and its importance should not be underestimated.

Fewer assemblies held Sunday Schools and Youth Clubs in 1988. 'The Brethren Today' survey of 1978 noted

28

What activities and services do you have?
All churches

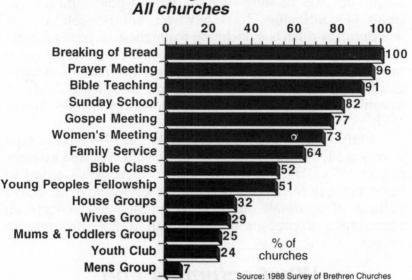

Figure 19: Activities and Services 1988

What activities and services do you have?
1978 v 1988

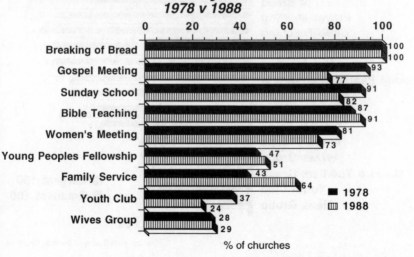

Figure 20: Activities and Services 1978 and 1988

that the number of children attending such activities appeared to be on the decline and the drop in numbers of assemblies still holding such activities would indicate this trend is continuing. It is however not possible to say whether this reflects a declining willingness of young people to participate in such activites, or a decline in resources and/ or commitment for such activities on the part of congregations. However, a slightly higher percentage (4%) of assemblies held Young People's fellowships in 1988 than in 1978.

Only 4 out of every 100 assemblies in 1988 did not hold a Prayer Meeting compared to 15 out of every 100 assemblies in 1978. The Prayer Meeting is now only second in importance to the Breaking of Bread service, as a distinctive feature of assembly activity. It presumably reflects an encouraging appreciation of the importance of corporate prayer.

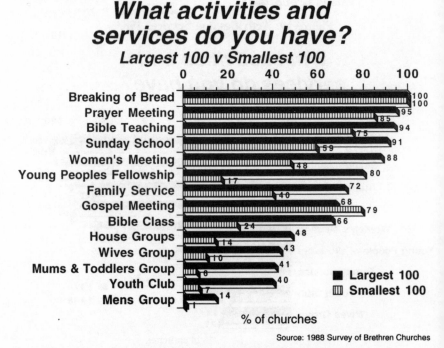

Source: 1988 Survey of Brethren Churches

Figure 21: Activities and Services 1988 by largest 100 and smallest 100 responding assemblies

Figure 21 shows that the largest 100 churches were more likely to be involved in the services and activities listed than the smallest 100 churches. For example, the largest assemblies were about 5 times more likely to hold a Youth Club or Young People's Fellowship and 7 times more likely to hold a Mums & Toddlers group than the smallest assemblies. This is not entirely surprising for the largest churches will have more resources at their disposal than the struggling smallest assemblies.

However, there was one exception: the Gospel Meeting was more likely to be held by one of the smallest assemblies (79%) than by one of the largest assemblies (68%). This perhaps indicates that the smallest churches as a group have continued to stick to the traditional pattern of activities, whereas the largest churches have introduced Family Services, Bible Classes, House groups, etc, in their pattern of activities.

It has already been noted that the largest churches saw a growth in membership between 1986 and 1988 whilst the smallest assemblies saw decline. A willingness to change and to be more attractive to outsiders could well be one of the main reasons for the comparative growth of the largest assemblies. Of course change is not easy for the smallest assemblies where resources are limited, but it may be the key to growth.

Teaching Meetings

Figure 22 shows that more than 2 in 3 Brethren assemblies had a systematic teaching programme in 1988. Increasingly Brethren assemblies are adopting systematic teaching for 'The Brethren Today' survey of 1978 showed that only 1 in 2 churches had a systematic ministry.

Around 6 in 7 Brethren assemblies had used pre-arranged speakers and/or outside speakers at their teaching meetings (Figure 23). Also a majority of Brethren assemblies had at some time invited non-Brethren speakers (55%) to their teaching meetings.

Nearly 2 in 3 assemblies had at some time used itinerant

Does the Church have Systematic Teaching?

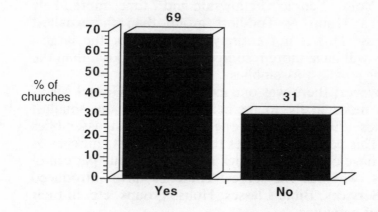

Source: 1988 Survey of Brethren Churches

Figure 22: Systematic Teaching in Assemblies 1988

At your teaching meetings do you ever have....?

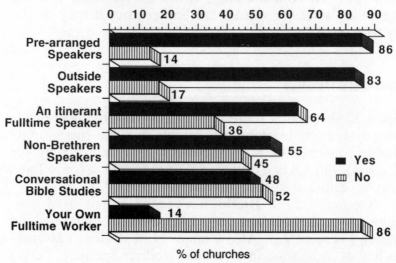

% of churches

Source: 1988 Survey of Brethren Churches

Figure 23: Possible features of teaching meetings

At how many of your teaching meetings would you ever have....?

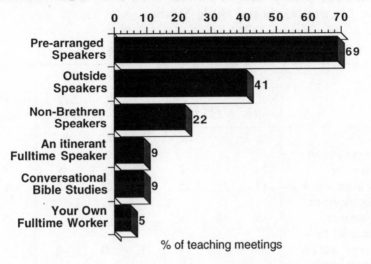

% of teaching meetings

Source: 1988 Survey of Brethren Churches

Figure 24: Regular features of teaching meetings

What proportion of teaching meetings have....?

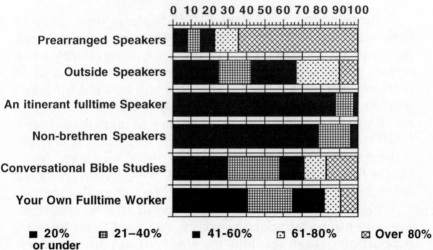

■ 20%   **⊞ 21–40%**   **■ 41-60%**   **⊡ 61-80%**   **⊠ Over 80%**
or under

Source: 1988 Survey of Brethren Churches

Figure 25: Proportions of teaching meetings with particular features

full-time speakers at their teaching meetings, but only 1 in 7 assemblies had use of their own full-time worker. In addition, nearly half of all Brethren assemblies had made use of conversational Bible Studies.

Table 4: Frequency of features at teaching meetings

| | Times per year | | | | | | |
	Not at all	1–10	11–20	21–30	31–49	Every Meeting	Average Number
	%	%	%	%	%	%	
Pre-arranged speaker	14	7	6	7	18	48	35
Outside speaker	17	21	15	19	25	3	20
Non-Brethren speaker	45	43	9	3	0	0	5
Itinerant full-time worker	36	56	7	1	0	0	5
Own resident full-time worker	86	6	3	2	3	0	3
Conversational Bible Study	52	14	14	6	7	7	11

Respondents were asked to indicate at how many of their teaching meetings in an average year they would use prearranged speakers, etc. For the responding churches as a whole, prearranged speakers will be present at 7 out of 10 teaching meetings. Outside speakers will be used for 2 in 5 teaching meetings and non-Brethren speakers for 1 in 10 meetings. Itinerant full-time speakers will take on average 1 in 10 teaching meetings and, perhaps surprisingly, resident full-time workers take as little as 1 in 20 meetings. More than a fifth of teaching meetings will involve conversational Bible Studies. Figure 24 illustrates these overall averages.

Figure 25 shows what proportion of Brethren assemblies who use prearranged speakers, etc, used them for what proportion of their teaching meetings. About three-quarters of teaching meetings have prearranged speakers, of whom over half are speakers from other Brethren assemblies.

Itinerant full-time speakers account for only a small proportion of teaching meetings, and so do non-Brethren speakers, although the latter are used more than the itinerants.

Figure 25 illustrates Table 4 which gives the percentage frequency of assemblies having a particular feature for teaching meetings, assuming 50 main meetings per year.

Teachers at meetings

Respondents were asked if they believed outside speakers were increasingly difficult to get. Figure 26 shows that a third of all assemblies found this to be true. It is perhaps a surprisingly high proportion as 4 in 9 assemblies disagreed. Why some assemblies find it increasingly difficult to get

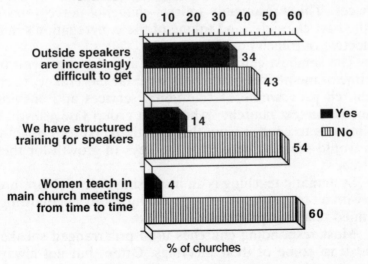

Figure 26: Statements about your assembly

outside speakers and other assemblies do not is not clear, but it may in part be possibly due to a shortage of Brethren speakers in some localities.

Only 1 in 7 Brethren assemblies had a structured training programme for speakers; the majority of assemblies had no structured training of any kind. Perhaps herein lies another reason why some assemblies found it increasingly difficult to get outside speakers for few new speakers are being trained.

Women in the main were not allowed to teach in main church meetings. Only in 1 in 25 assemblies were women allowed to teach from time to time.

Summary

There were some significant changes in main activities between 1978 and 1988. The Gospel Meeting although still held by more than 3 in 4 assemblies, has declined from the second most-frequently-held meeting in 1978 to the fifth most-frequently-held meeting in 1988. In contrast, by 1988 an *extra* 1 in 5 Brethren assemblies were holding family services. This presumably reflects changing perceptions as to the best character and timing of the congregation's main collective outreach activity.

The smallest churches which as a group experienced a decline in membership numbers were far more likely to run a church programme of traditional services and activities than the largest churches which as a group saw growth. A willingness to change from this traditional pattern of activities would seem to be one of the keys to growth for these churches.

Systematic teaching is an increasing aspect of Brethren life with a large majority of responding churches following a planned teaching programme in 1988.

Most responding churches used prearranged speakers in at least some of their meetings. Often, but not always, prearranged speakers will be used as part of the systematic teaching programme. Although a majority of speakers arranged beforehand will be members of that particular fellowship, outside speakers including non-Brethren speakers, will also be used from time to time by many assemblies.

Only a small minority of responding churches had a structural training programme for speakers and this may lead to a shortage of trained speakers in the future.

5

Evangelistic Methods

The traditional Gospel Meeting still remains the most frequently used evangelistic method even though 'The Brethren Today' survey of 1978 found it did not attract large numbers of non-members. However, more and more assemblies are abandoning this evangelistic method in favour of others (more than 90% of assemblies used the Gospel Meeting in 1978).

More than 6 in 9 assemblies used door-to-door visitations as an evangelistic method in 1988 compared to only 4 in 9 in 1978. Open air work was used by 1 in 5 assemblies in 1988 compared to only 1 in 10 in 1978, whilst half the assemblies were involved in adult evangelism (Figure 27). Increasingly Brethren assemblies are recognising the need to get out into the community and not expect the community to come to them.

This recognition of the need to be more outward looking perhaps explains why the Family Service, although seen as being more successful in attracting non-members than the Gospel Meeting ('The Brethren Today' survey of 1978), had not significantly increased its popularity as an evangelistic method between 1978 and 1988—other methods were being used instead.

The traditional Gospel Meeting was by far the most important evangelistic method used by the smallest churches in 1988. In contrast a majority of the largest churches, in addition to the Gospel Meeting, made use of door-to-door visitation, calendar/guest services (for exam-

What evangelistic methods are used by your church?

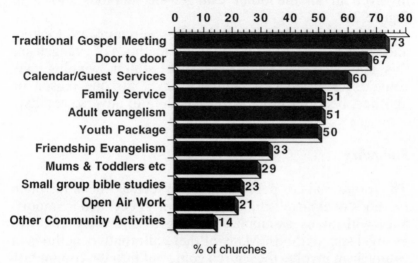

% of churches

Source: 1988 Survey of Brethren Churches

Figure 27: Evangelistic methods used

What evangelistic methods are used by your church?
Largest 100 v Smallest 100

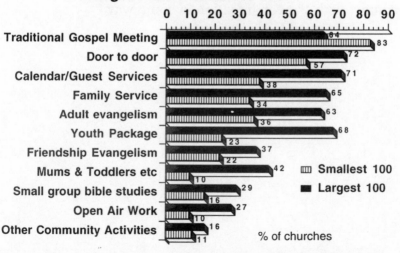

% of churches

Source: 1988 Survey of Brethren Churches

Figure 28: Evangelistic methods used by size of assembly

ple, Christmas services), Family Services, youth work and adult evangelism. They were also far more likely to be involved in all the other evangelistic methods shown in Figure 28.

As a group, the largest churches were outward looking and willing to try new and different methods of evangelism; this approach has been very successful in winning new converts. The smallest churches have, for one reason or another, been far more insular leading to adverse results.

Summary

The traditional Gospel Meeting, still seen as one of the main methods of evangelism, has nevertheless declined in importance with many assemblies seeking to find more effective evangelistic methods. Many of these alternative methods of evangelism involve the church going out into the community rather than waiting for non-members to come to church.

The survey did not ask however about the *effectiveness* of contact or friendship evangelism, and mothers and toddlers' groups etc, in leading to those conversions which did take place, nor did it seek to explore the extent to which conversions were drawn from those already in regular contact with the congregation in some way.

6

Leadership

Types of Leadership

Respondents were asked to indicate what form of leadership their assembly had; the results are shown in Figure 29.

Most Brethren assemblies in 1988, as they did in 1978, had an eldership or oversight. Interestingly, though, 21 of the smallest 100 churches did not, perhaps reflecting their small-ness and the effective involvement of all (male) members of leadership. In 1978, 1 in 4 assemblies had deacons and by 1988 this proportion had risen to 1 in 3 assemblies. If this trend continues around half the assemblies should have deacons by the turn of the century. Indeed, 50 of the largest 100 churches already have deacons, and this proportion is likely to increase.

Although a small minority of assemblies had a Brothers' Meeting as the form of leadership, the proportion of assemblies run in this way has halved from 15% in 1978 to only 7% in 1988. There is a clear trend therefore towards leadership by officially recognised individuals, and towards having spiritual and practical tasks discharged by distinct groups.

None of the largest 100 churches had a Brothers' Meeting as the form of leadership. A further 1 in 8 assemblies also had committees as part of their leadership structure, with the largest assemblies twice as likely to have committees than other assemblies.

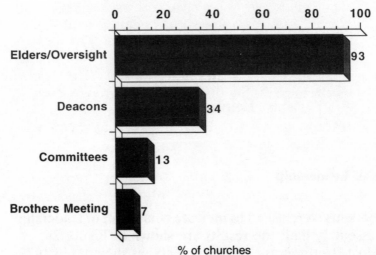

What form of leadership does the church have?

Figure 29: Types of assembly leadership

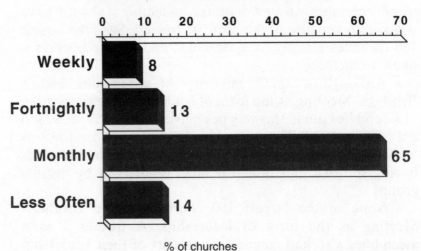

How often does the leadership team meet?

Figure 30: Frequency with which the Leadership Team meets

Leadership Meetings

A majority of Brethren assemblies had a monthly meeting
for their leadership team and this has changed little since
1978. However, 1 in 6 assemblies held weekly or fortnightly
leadership meetings in 1988, an increase on 1978 (1 in 9
assemblies), probably reflecting changed perceptions of the
burdens and needs of pastoral leadership. The largest
churches were more likely than other Brethren assemblies
to hold their leadership meetings on a weekly or fortnightly
basis in contrast to the smallest churches who were more
likely to hold them less frequently. The overall picture is
reflected in Figure 30.

One Brethren assembly in 5 said that their leadership
team went on special retreats and one assembly also in 5
said their leadership met together with the elders of other
local Brethren assemblies from time to time (Figure 31).
However, this was in part dependent upon the size of the
assembly. Three in 8 of the largest 100 assemblies said their
leadership team attended special retreats compared to only
1 in 20 of the smallest 100 assemblies, and 1 in 4 of the
largest 100 assemblies met with other elderships compared
to 1 in 7 of the smallest 100 assemblies.

Appointment of Leaders

In two-thirds of Brethren assemblies new elders and
deacons were chosen solely by the current members of the
leadership team. In a further quarter of assemblies members
of the leadership team still appointed new leaders but did so
in consultation with other members of the congregation.
Only a small minority of assemblies (1 in 20) appointed
leaders by elections in the church or through some other
means (Figure 32).

Women in Leadership

Table 5 shows that women had a leadership role only in a
minority of Brethren assemblies, usually serving on a church

Does the leadership team attend...?

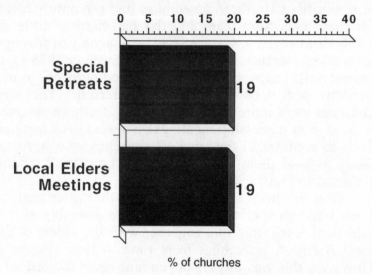

% of churches

Source: 1988 Survey of Brethren Churches

Figure 31: Meetings attended by the Leadership

How is the leadership chosen?

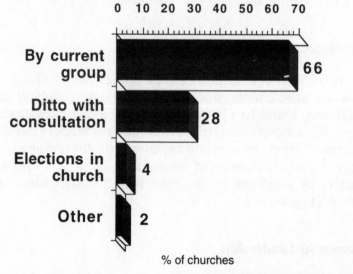

% of churches

Source: 1988 Survey of Brethren Churches

Figure 32: How the Leadership is chosen

committee (3 in 10 assemblies). A few served as deacons or
elders. Woman elders occur in the smallest rather than the
largest churches, probably reflecting the overall availability
of leadership gifts in such churches. Generally, however,

Table 5: Women in leadership

Type of leadership where women serve	100 largest assemblies	100 smallest assemblies	All assemblies
Elders	0%	2%	1%
Deacons	19%	4%	13%
Church Committees	40%	16%	30%

The total column is illustrated in Figure 33.

women were more likely to serve in the larger assemblies via
the committee mechanism. This is probably partly because
that is not perceived as raising theological questions.
Whether this female involvement in leadership causes
growth, or growth allows the freedom (and perhaps creates
the greater need) for women leaders is not known.

Paid Workers

One fifth (20%) of the responding assemblies had a full-time
or part-time resident worker in 1988, more than double the
proportion (9%) who had a resident worker in 1978. Of
those who did have a resident worker a majority (3 in 5) had
a full-time worker. Added to this, a *further* 1 in 7 assemblies
believed there was a future possibility of appointing a full-
time worker (Figure 34).

Whether a Brethren assembly employed a worker was
dependent in part upon the size of the assembly, probably
reflecting resources as well as attitudes. For example, a
quarter of the largest churches employed a full-time worker
compared to only 4% of the smallest assemblies who
presumably lack the finances to do so.

Women play a leadership role as.....

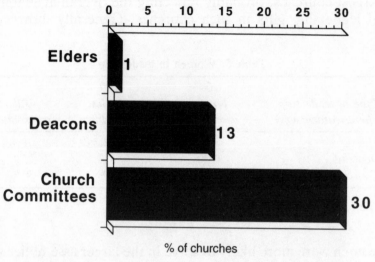

Figure 33: Assemblies with women in leadership

The church has....

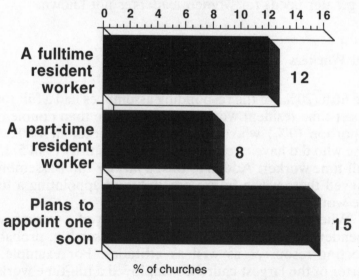

Figure 34: Assemblies with resident workers

The Church has...

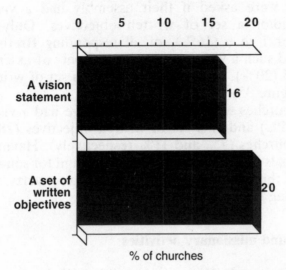

Figure 35: Assemblies with vision statement and/or written objectives

Does the church have any .....

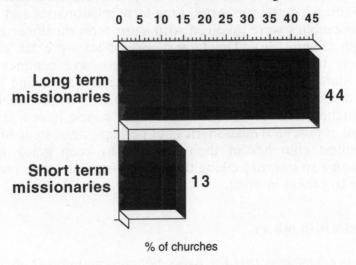

Figure 36: Assemblies with missionaries

Objectives

Respondents were asked if their assembly had a vision statement and/or a set of written objectives. Only 47 assemblies, or 1 in 6 (16%), of all responding Brethren assembles had such a vision statement and only 61 assemblies, or 1 in 5 (20%), of all assemblies had a set of written objectives Figure 35).

Large churches were more likely to have had a vision statement (25%) and/or a set of written objectives (28%) than small churches (7% and 11% respectively). Having a clear set of goals to aim for could in part account for some of the success of the largest assemblies in gaining converts, and indeed in being larger assemblies at all!

Missionaries and missionary activities

A large majority of Brethren assemblies (3 in 4) hold regular missionary activities. This was more true of the largest churches (6 in 7 had regular activities) and less true of the smallest churches (2 in 3 assemblies).

A substantial minority (4 in 9) of Brethren assemblies commended and supported long term missionaries and 1 in 8 assemblies were involved with short term missionaries in 1988 (Figure 36). The largest assemblies were far more likely than the smallest assemblies to have commended missionaries, 7 in 10 of the largest churches having long term missionaries compared to only 1 in 4 of the smallest churches. The largest churches will of course have a larger pool of potential missionaries but perhaps, also, some of the smallest churches in their struggle to keep going have become so inward looking they have forgotten how to reach out to others in need.

Links with others

Figure 37 shows that the overwhelming majority (6 in 7) of Brethren assemblies have links with other assemblies. A further 6 in 10 assemblies had links with other evangelical churches; larger assemblies were more likely to have such links than smaller assemblies.

A small minority of assemblies had links with the local Council of Churches or the Evangelical Alliance (1 in 6). Again larger assemblies were more likely to have links with these organisations than smaller assemblies. Only one per cent of Brethren assemblies had links with the British Council of Churches.

'Charismatic' Gifts

Only a very small minority of Brethren assemblies said that the characteristic 'charismatic' gifts of Tongues, Prophecy and Healing took place in church meetings. Only 12 assemblies reported Tongues, 23 assemblies reported Prophecy and 20 reported Healing (Figure 38). 'The Brethren Today' survey of 1978 found that 3 in 4 assemblies believed that such charismatic activities should not be allowed in church meetings; perhaps this is still true today.

Summary

Most Brethren assemblies still have an eldership or oversight as their form of church government. However, more assemblies had introduced deacons as part of the leadership structure between 1978 and 1988. New leaders are, across the Brethren movement as a whole, usually appointed solely by the members of the current leadership team, though sometimes there is consultation with church members as a whole. There is some evidence of changing patterns in leadership work, though a small majority of the responding churches retained monthly oversight meetings in 1988.

An increasing number of assemblies are appointing full-time or part-time resident workers. Insofar as women are allowed a part in leadership, it is likely to be as a member of a church committee in a larger church. Only a small minority of assemblies have a vision statement and/or a set of written objectives.

Does the church have links with...

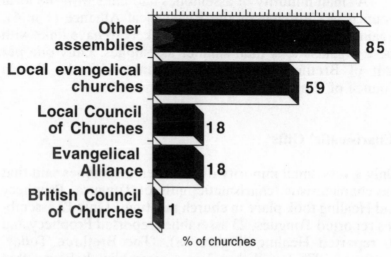

Source: 1988 Survey of Brethren Churches

Figure 37: Assemblies with links to other churches

In the meetings of the church do any of the following take place.....

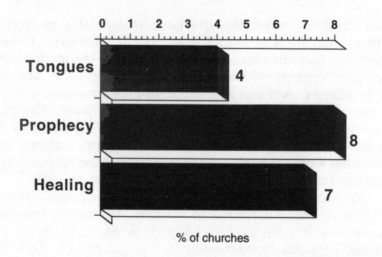

% of churches

Source: 1988 Survey of Brethren Churches

Figure 38: Assemblies with charismatic gifts

Many Brethren assemblies hold regular missionary activities and a substantial minority commended and supported long term missionaries. Larger assemblies tended to have more involvement with missionaries than smaller assemblies who struggle to keep their own fellowships going. A majority of Brethren assemblies had links with other assemblies and with other evangelical churches.

The 'Charismatic' movement does not seem yet to have made a major impact on the Brethren movement although a very small minority of assemblies did allow 'charismatic' gifts to be used in church meetings.

7
Assembly Features by Size

Throughout this evaluation of the 1988 survey reference has been made to the differences between the results for the one hundred largest and one hundred smallest assemblies in the responding sample. To gain an impression of what these assemblies are like, a list follows (Table 6) of the features of these three types of assemblies.

A majority of the largest assemblies were growing assemblies between 1983 and 1988 and on average added 4 new members per assembly between 1986 and 1988. In contrast a majority of the smallest assemblies were in decline between 1983 and 1988 losing on average one member per assembly between 1986 and 1988. The middle sized assemblies had a similar proportion of both growing and declining assemblies between 1983 and 1988 and gained 1½ new members per assembly between 1986 and 1988 following the overall pattern for the responding churches.

What does the future hold for the middle sized assemblies? Will they show an increasing tendency towards decline as seen by the smallest assemblies or towards healthy growth as experienced by the largest assemblies? Encouragingly the middle sized assemblies tended towards the largest assemblies with a substantial minority of them seeing 5 or more conversions between 1986 and 1988, but the follow through to baptism needs to be improved. If the trend in conversions continues and the number of baptisms is improved the middle sized assemblies should continue to see some overall growth in the future.

Table 6: Features by size of assemblies

Feature	Largest hundred assemblies	Middle sized assemblies	Smallest hundred assemblies	All assemblies
1983–1988				
% of growing churches	52%	40%	25%	39%
% of declining churches	31%	43%	58%	44%
1986–1988				
Actual increase/decrease per assembly	+3.9	+1.5	−1.1	+1.4
% of assemblies with no conversions	14%	23%	51%	29%
% of assemblies with 5 plus conversions	51%	40%	11%	34%
% of assemblies with no baptisms	10%	21%	55%	29%
% of assemblies with 5 plus baptisms	55%	28%	4%	29%
Average number of activities and services per assembly	9.4	9.2	5.7	8.1
Average number of evangelistic methods used per assembly	5.5	5.2	3.4	4.7
% of assemblies with elders/oversight	97%	100%	79%	93%
% of assemblies with deacons	50%	37%	15%	34%
% of assemblies with female deacons	19%	16%	4%	13%
% of assemblies with at least one full-time leader	23%	9%	4%	12%
% of assemblies with long-term missionaries	70%	39%	24%	44%

Middle sized assemblies were far more likely, as were the largest assemblies, to hold a wide variety of activities and services and use different types of evangelistic methods than the smallest assemblies. They were also more likely than the smallest assemblies to have introduced deacons into the leadership structure, and almost as likely as the largest assemblies to have had female deacons. This willingness to introduce change could be a key towards their possible future growth.

However, like the smallest assemblies, they were far less likely than the largest assemblies to have had their own resident full-time worker or to have commended and supported a long term missionary. This could perhaps be due to a perceived lack of financial resources to do so.

8

The English Church Census

Introduction

The English Church Census took place on 15th October 1989 when all the 38,607 churches in *England* were invited to complete a form asking information about attendance and other items. Naturally the churches of the Christian (Open) Brethren were included, but unfortunately only 38% responded. 35% of the Closed Christian Brethren (largely No 4's) responded, their addresses having been obtained from the list of premises available for Registered marriages. A copy of the questionnaire used is given in the published results 'Prospects for the Nineties' (MARC Europe, London, 1991).

The Brethren were included as part of the Independent Sector, one of the two Sectors that saw especial growth in attendance in the late 1980's (the other was the Pentecostal).

The Independent Sector

The Open Brethren as they will be called here for simplicity remained fairly static in attendance terms in the 1980's, whilst others in the Independent Sector grew. Consequently the proportion of the Open Brethren in the Independent sector shrank from 21% in 1979 to 15% by 1989. Table 7 gives the details.

Table 7: Proportions of adult churchgoers by denomination within Independent churches 1975–1989

Denomination/group	1979*	1985	1989	Response rate
	%	%	%	%
FIEC	20	24	22	73
Congregational Federation	4	3	3	72
EFCC	3	3	2	71
House Church Movement	22	31	37	70
UEC	1	–	–	65
Churches of Christ	2	1	1	51
Residential Schools	17	12	11	49
Christian Brethren (Open)	21	16	15	38
Christian Brethren (Closed)	3	3	3	35
All Others	7	7	6	63
Total (= 100%)	0.21m	0.26m	0.29m	58

* Estimate based on membership figures.

The Independent churches attendance experience has been quite different from the rest of the Free Churches, with growth rather than decline being the order of the day. As a consequence they have moved from 14% of the total in 1975 to 23% in 1989. Table 8 gives details.

Table 8: Changes in adult churchgoing of the Independent churches and the rest of the Free Churches 1975–1989

Church	1975	C	1979	C	1985	C	1989
		%		%		%	
Independent Churches	167,000	+23	206,000	+25	257,500	+14	292,800
All Other Free Churches	1,042,000		1,041,000	–7	972,200	–2	956,200
Total Free Churches	1,209,000	+3	1,247,000	–1	1,229,700	+2	1,249,000

C = Percentage change.

The actual numbers of churchgoers for the various groups and denominations are given in Table 9.

Table 9: Components of Independent churches 1979–1989

Denomination/Group	Adult churchgoers 1979*	Adult churchgoers 1985	Adult churchgoers 1989	Percentage change 1979–89	1989 as percentage of adult population
				%	%
FIEC	43,400	60,900	63,400	+46	0.14
Congregational Federation	8,700	9,000	9,400	+8 }	0.04
EFCC	6,400	6,600	6,800	+6 }	
House Church Movement	44,400	81,000	108,500	+144	0.30
UEC	1,400	1,000	1,000	−29 }	
Churches of Christ	3,900	3,200	3,300	−15 }	0.08
Residential Schools	32,300	31,300	31,000	−4 }	
Christian Brethren (Open)	44,000	41,300	43,500	−1 }	0.13
Christian Brethren (Closed)	7,000	7,300	7,600	+9 }	
All Others	14,500	15,900	18,300	+26	0.06
Total	206,000	257,500	292,800	+42	0.75

* Estimate based on membership figures.

Projecting the Open Brethren figures back to 1975 gives an adult attendance of 43,600, and forwards to 1995 of 42,000 and to 2000 of 41,600. The Closed Brethren are respectively 6,700 in 1975 and 7,900 in 1995 and 8,200 in 2000. It can be seen that compared with some other groups in the Independent Sector, the Open Brethren attendance has varied slightly more, as Figure 39 indicates (where the 1989–2000 figures are estimates represented by a different shading).

Churchmanship

One feature of the English Church Census was to give respondents (usually the minister or leading elder) an opportunity to indicate the type of churchmanship of that particular church. Brethren leaders gave such information for their assemblies, which showed them to be mainly evangelical, but not entirely so. Table 10 gives details of

Adult Churchgoers in some of the Independent Groups

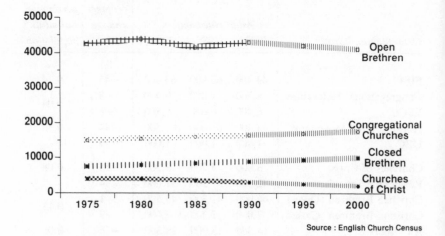

Source : English Church Census

Figure 39: Adult churchgoers in some of the Independent groups

their strengths, and how they changed between 1985 and 1989.

Table 10: Churchmanship of Open Brethren adults

Type	Strength in 1989	How changed 1985–1989
Evangelical	91% or 39,600	Increased 6%
Low Church	7% or 3,100	Decreased 1%
Broad/Liberal	1% or 400	Decreased 10%
All others	1% or 400	Decreased 13%
Overall	100% or 43,500	Increased 5%

Exactly what those replying understood by 'low church' is not clear. Generally it applies to a major group within the Church of England, but it is likely that Brethren churches ticking that category meant their church was open to

allcomers. Any ticking both Low Church and Evangelical
were counted simply as Low Church.

The Evangelical group broke down further as shown in
Table 11.

Table 11: Churchmanship of Open Brethren Evangelical adults

Type	Strength in 1989	How changed 1985–1989
Mainstream Evangelical	90% or 35,600	Increased 3%
Charismatic Evangelical	8% or 3,200	Increased 74%
Broad Evangelical	2% or 800	Increased 6%
All Evangelicals	100% or 39,600	Increased 6%

It is quite clear that the bulk of Open Brethren are
solidly of the mainstream evangelical persuasion—biblical,
witnessing Christians, progressive perhaps, but not charismatic. It is however the charismatic sector which is growing—and fast. They numbered about 1,800 in 1985 and grew
to 3,200 by 1989, a very significant growth. Why is this
group growing so much in Open Brethren assemblies? The
charismatics have grown generally across the denominations, but nowhere as fast as with the Open Brethren,
although the numbers here are relatively small thus making
high percentage changes easier to attain.

Environment

In what types of area are Open Brethren churches situated?
Eight types were given on the Census form, but are here
summarised into four main categories.

Table 12: Environment of Open Brethren adults

Type	Strength in 1989	How changed 1985–1989
Suburban/urban fringe	52% or 22,600	Increased 6%
Towns	27% or 11,700	Increased 4%
Rural area	13% or 5,700	Decreased 7%
City Centre/Inner City	8% or 3,500	Increased 33%
Overall	100% or 43,500	Increased 5%

One Open Brethren adult in two in England worships in a suburban or urban fringe setting. One in four worships in a separate town. Both these categories grew slightly in the late 1980s. Rural area attendance—one in eight—decreased however, a trend *against* experience in other denominations. Do people moving into rural, often commuter, areas tend to go only to the Anglican churches? Are rural Brethren churches likely to be of a character which does not attract Brethren attenders from urban, or suburban churches when they move to rural areas? Are such people likely to turn to Brethren assemblies should they tire of the Church of England (especially as most rural Anglican churches are not evangelical)?

It is the City Centre churches where major growth was experienced in the late 1980s—from 2,600 in 1985 to 3,500 by 1989. What generated such growth? Alas, the Census does not tell us.

Morning and Evening attendance

The Open Brethren expect adults to go to church twice on a Sunday. Other denominations teach similarly, but the Brethren see more people going to church morning and evening than most other groups. The Pentecostals with 48% of 'twicers' are higher than the Brethren, and the Afro-Caribbeans at 41% very close behind, but these three lead the field in repeated attendance. The actual figures are shown in Table 13.

Table 13: Occasions of adult attendance on a Sunday

| Open Brethren | Once only | | Twice: Morning and Evening |
	Morning	Evening	
1989	31%	26%	43%
1985	25%	32%	43%
All churches			
1989	61%	25%	14%
1985	59%	25%	16%

The Open Brethren are seeing more people going to church only once on a Sunday, going in the morning rather than the evening, though the proportion going twice has remained constant in 1985 and 1989. Is that because people appreciate the Breaking of Bread service and dislike the Gospel Meeting in the evening? Or is it simply a reflection of a general sociological shift towards church attendances on Sunday morning rather than evening in many areas? Those going twice on a Sunday are about three times as many as in churches generally showing a very high level of commitment. How can that commitment be used in other ways?

Growth of Open Brethren churches

The answers to the Census allow an analysis by size, and a comparison of the Census and the 1988 Survey has been given in Table 2, which showed little significant difference between the two, though the English Census had more larger assemblies giving details.

Growth in the assemblies increased with size, as Table 14 shows with the overall figure not significantly different from the 39% found in the 1988 study.

Table 14: Growth of Open Brethren churches 1985–1989 by size

Size of Assembly	Percentage that size	Percentage which grew
25 or under	31%	10%
26 – 50	27%	20%
51 – 75	17%	48%
76 – 100	13%	65%
101 – 150	8%	67%
Over 150	4%	76%
Overall	100%	34%

Whilst some smaller, under 50, assemblies grew, there was a significant jump in the percentage which grew with assemblies of size 51–75 when nearly half saw growth in the late 1980s, and with assemblies 76 or over when two-thirds or more grew in the same period. Which comes first—does size help growth, or does growth increase size? Probably both, but neither says much about *why* growth came—a factor which needs more research.

But irrespective of the reason, the fact of the matter is that growing assemblies are relatively few. Those 76 or over are only one-quarter of all assemblies—so how do growing larger assemblies best use their resources and manpower to help smaller static or declining assemblies? The need to share between assemblies emerges from such figures, and is a question that is important to answer if the movement as a whole is to grow. It is an issue which the Brethren have not previously appeared to solve well, and perhaps the challenge of these Census figures is to consider how to regain a sense of Christian brotherhood. Giving help requires time and energy and willingness, receiving help requires humility and patience and also willingness. Progressive assemblies need to partner with others for the sake not of the Brethren movement but for the Kingdom of God. Such a path is not easy, but it is suggested it be earnestly tried.

Age of Open Brethren

The Census also asked the gender and age-group of those present. 42% of Open Brethren adults were men, the same percentage as in churches throughout England. The age breakdown is given in Table 15, compared with the population figures.

This table highlights the following:

* Brethren have more girls (under 15) than boys, and more girls but fewer boys proportionately than the population. Other churches manage to have more boys. How can the Brethren attract more?

* Brethren hold their teenagers rather better than other churches, though the Independent churches generally are good with teens.

* Like many other denominations the Brethren are especially

**Table 15: Open Brethren and population by age-group
and gender 1989**

	Open Brethren			Population		
	Men	*Women*	*Total*	*Men*	*Women*	*Total*
Under 15	9%	12%	21%	10%	9%	19%
15–19	4%	5%	9%	4%	4%	8%
20–29	5%	6%	11%	8%	8%	16%
30–44	7%	9%	16%	10%	10%	20%
45–64	9%	11%	20%	11%	11%	22%
65 or over	8%	15%	23%	6%	9%	15%
All ages	42%	58%	100%	49%	51%	100%

weak with people in their twenties, both men and women.
How are the young marrieds to be attracted?

* Brethren are weaker than the population figures would
  suggest amongst those aged 30 to 64, especially men. How
  can the Brethren attract older men?

* The Brethren however manage to have good numbers of
  older men (65 or over) and women. Is this part of a
  generation used to attending church?

The total proportion of people 65 or over is very high,
much higher than most denominations, although not as high
as the Methodists or United Reformed Church. Such higher
numbers of elderly people mean that many will die in the
years 1989–2000. Assuming that the normal English mortal-
ity experience applies to the Open Brethren (and it may not
since many do not smoke or drink alcohol), then some 10%
of existing attendance can be expected to pass on in this
eleven year period. In other words, the Brethren have to
grow 10% in these 11 years *just to stand still*. The numbers
dying are illustrated in Figure 40.

Summary

What then are the main conclusions to be drawn from the
English Church Census for the Open Brethren?

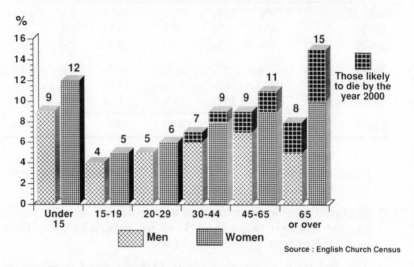

Figure 40: Age of those attending Open Brethren Assemblies 1989
and those likely to die by the year 2000

1) Whilst the Brethren are naturally part of the Independent Movement, they have not grown as have others in
the movement in the 1980s. The lack of growth is not due
to the Brethren not being largely charismatic for the
FIEC churches are not charismatic by and large either,
but have seen growth. It is important to discover the
factors inhibiting such growth.

2) The Brethren are largely both evangelical and mainstream evangelical. What does this mean in practice?
Whilst there has been overall growth 1985–1989 the
charismatic wing has seen spectacular growth in this
period, though they are only a small part of the whole
movement. What can they share with others? What can
the non-charismatics learn from the charismatics?

3) Brethren in built-up areas generally have seen growth,

but those in rural areas have seen decline. How can those likely to be smaller, more isolated, and perhaps more independent, find fellowship with neighbouring assemblies in stronger positions? A regional framework of some kind might seem desirable.

4) The Brethren tradition of attending church morning and evening is holding strong. How can they use this strength to best effect? There is a tendency for some to switch to the morning service however, and the implications of this need to be worked out by each local assembly.

5) Growth of assemblies is much more likely the larger the assembly, especially if over 50 or 75 people. These larger assemblies need to help the smaller assemblies—perhaps by 'adopting' them, sharing resources and caring for them in practical and prayerful ways.

6) The age breakdown of Brethren attending church is worrying. The proportions of elderly Brethren mean that relatively many deaths will occur in the 1990s. This will hit smaller assemblies particularly hard—how can their closure be prevented?

7) The Brethren lack folk in their twenties and men of working age. What are the main attractions of the Brethren and how can they be applied to people in these groups? The Bishop of Southwark said recently, 'We have moved from where Christianity is culture to where Christianity is choice'. This applies to Brethren assemblies as well as Anglican churches. Why should someone choose to attend a Brethren assembly? What do they offer? And if that is felt an improper question, what alternative question can be posed to lead to equal action?

9

Trends and Comparisons with Other Christian Groupings 1960–1990

The previous chapter made some comparisons between the experience of Open Brethren assemblies in recent years and that of other groups of independent churches. The purpose of this chapter is to explore such comparisons across Christian groups as a whole in the UK, and particularly with relevant groups of independent churches, in relation to certain key variables in church life—those variables being determined by the availability of relevant data.

As noted in Appendix 1, the Christian Brethren in the British Isles were probably at the peak of their numerical strength, both of congregations and membership, in 1959. The calculation of total membership was based on uncertain data on the average membership of congregations. For more recent years, some data on average membership are available from the surveys of Brethren churches undertaken in 1966, 1978 and 1988, and from the English Church Census. They suggest an average of 45 in 1966 (sample size: 75)[1]; 50 in 1978 (sample size: 249), though this number included children attending services as well as adults[2]; and 52 in 1988 (sample size: 308). A separate estimate for

---

1 Graham D Brown, 'How can we improve our evangelism? Deductions from a Survey of Assemblies' in *Christian Brethren Research Fellowship Journal*, No. 21, May 1971, pp. 44–57.
2 Graham Brown and Brian Mills, *'The Brethren'* Today: A Factual Survey, Exeter: The Christian Brethren Research Fellowship, 1980.

Scotland in 1989 suggested an average of 50 for the 254 Brethren congregations then thought to be in existence.[3] These figures may be compared with the average *attendance* for the Open Brethren congregations responding to the English Church Census of [45],[4] a figure which is not necessarily inconsistent with a membership of around 50.

These figures cannot give certainty about average congregational size for the United Kingdom as a whole because of the possibility of geographical bias among the churches responding to the various surveys. But on alternative assumptions about congregational size, total membership of the Christian Brethren in the United Kingdom, based on the numbers of congregations given in the various address lists, might be as shown in Table 16.

**Table 16: Christian Brethren membership 1970–1991
by congregational size**

Assumed congregation size	*1970*	*1975*	*1983*	*1991*	*1991 as % of 1970*
40	67,440	66,240	62,200	55,200 }	
45	75,870	74,520	69,975	62,100 }	82%
50	84,300	82,800	77,750	69,000 }	

Membership by country, on the assumption of an average congregational size of 50 not varying between countries, might be as shown in Table 17.

Overall, these figures suggest a pattern of rapid and steady decline since the 1960s.[5] Since 1970, total numbers of

3 Information supplied by Neil Dickson (Kilmarnock).
4 See above figures in Tables 1 and 9.
5 An interesting sidelight from the printed lists for the period is the gradual change in the way congregations describe themselves and their church buildings. In 1959 only 4% of Brethren buildings in England and Wales were terms other than 'gospel hall' or 'hall' or 'mission hall'. In Scotland the percentage was negligible. By 1970 19% of congregations in England and Wales were describing themselves as 'church' or 'Evangelical church' or similarly; so were 4% of congregations in Scotland. By 1983, these percentages were 32% and 8% respectively, and by the 1991 list they were 42% and 15% respectively.

Table 17: Christian Brethren membership by country within UK

	1970	1975	1983	1991
England	55,950	54,250	50,950	43,550
Wales	5,000	5,250	5,350	4,650
Scotland	14,800	14,950	13,700	12,550
N. Ireland	8,550	8,350	7,750	8,250
Total	84,300	82,800	77,750	69,000

Christian Brethren have probably declined by almost a fifth (18%). This figure chimes with what many observers would sense has been occurring during the period.

In this respect, the Christian Brethren have not been exceptional. In general, the last two decades have seen a decline in church-going and in the number of congregations in the United Kingdom. The position is summarised in the lastest edition of *British Social Trends since 1900*[6]: Over the last 15 years British church membership has declined from 8.5 million to just under 7 million [including Roman Catholic attendance at mass]. In the same period the number of full-time ministers has decreased by 4,000, and 3,000 church buildings have been closed.'[6] Successive editions of the *UK Christian Handbook* suggests a total decline in church membership in the UK between 1970 and 1990 of some 23% with the greater part of the reduction occurring in the 1970s.

Many however would not be content with this general comparison: they would feel that the position of the Christian Brethren ought to be compared with a narrower range of avowedly Evangelical nonconformist groups, in particular Evangelical Baptists, FIEC churches, and the New and House churches.

Table 18 opposite (again compiled from the data in the *UK Christian Handbooks*) illustrates trends in church membership between 1970 and 1990 for the main denominational groups. The rates of decline have been fairly uniform for the Anglican, Roman Catholic, Methodist and Presby-

---

6 *Op. cit.*, p. 522.

Table 18: Denominational membership in the UK, 1970–1990

	1970	1975	1980	1985	1987	1990	1990 as % of 1970	1990 as % of 1980
Anglican	2,547,767	2,270,028	2,153,854	1,985,367	1,927,506	1,838,659	72	85
Methodist	694,333	614,729	541,773	503,822	516,739	483,387	70	89
Presbyterian	1,806,736	1,645,548	1,508,509	1,385,992	1,346,366	1,291,672	71	86
Roman Catholic	2,714,520	2,534,395	2,342,264	2,120,830	2,059,240	1,945,626	72	83
Baptist	295,341	270,259	239,874	243,736	241,451	241,842	82	101
of which Baptist Union	272,002	249,481	216,979	213,773	213,748	210,412	77	97
Other Baptist	23,333	20,778	22,895	29,963	27,703	31,430	135	137
Reformed churches	160,474	144,872	138,757	135,881	132,652	138,195	86	100
of which FIEC	20,760	19,820	21,923	30,150	30,260	33,000	159	151
House & other denoml.	100	12,000	25,000	95,000	130,000	190,000	100,000	760
Pentecostal/Holiness	91,430	83,742	89,066	79,169	92,549	95,663	105	107
Afro-Caribbean	32,317	47,410	65,176	65,900	66,511	69,658	216	107
Salvation Army	91,799	92,661	74,505	59,108	55,942	62,063	68	83
Christian Brethren	75,870	74,520	71,685	66,000	63,180	63,200	83	88
All other denominations	267,029	274,218	281,110	305,648	377,874	394,476	148	140
TOTAL	8,781,855	8,062,862	7,527,888	7,046,453	6,926,830	6,764,441	77	90

Table 19: Numbers of Christian congregations in the UK, 1970–1990

	1970	1975	1980	1985	1987	1990	1990 as % of 1970	1990 as % of 1980
Anglican	20,334	19,788	19,381	18,905	18,713	18,278	90	94
Roman Catholic	5,096	4,111	4,135	4,368	4,390	4,457	87	108
Methodist	9,998	9,138	8,557	8,022	7,787	7,500	75	88
Presbyterian	6,633	6,368	6,108	5,655	5,637	5,503	83	90
Baptist	3,678	3,619	3,344	3,375	3,433	3,439	94	103
of which Baptist Union	3,133	3,052	2,762	2,751	2,793	2,788	89	101
Other Baptist	545	567	582	624	634	651	119	112
Reformed churches	1,736	1,844	1,882	1,791	1,755	1,700	98	90
of which FIEC	394	415	443	437	432	423	107	95
House churches*	1	180	340	1,150	2,100	3,400	340,000	1000
Pentecostal/Holiness	1,133	1,180	1,213	1,245	1,261	1,286	114	106
Afro-Caribbean	574	697	844	896	924	965	168	114
Salvation Army	1,900	1,840	1,750	1,560	1,550	1,537	81	88
Christian Brethren†	1,065	1,000	952	1,010	952	923	87	97
All other denominations	1,382	1,437	1,480	1,853	1,671	1,936	140	131
TOTAL	53,530	51,202	49,986	49,830	50,173	50,924	95	102

Notes: * And other non-denominational churches; † UK Christian Handbook figures.

terian denominations, with an overall reduction of 28% over the decades, and of 15% in the 1980s. The experience of the Evangelical groups has been more variable however. They fall broadly into three groups: those which were static or moderately declining in the 1970s with signs of stabilisation or a reduction in the rate of decline in the 1980s (the Baptist Union churches; the Pentecostal/Holiness churches; and the reformed groups with the exception of the FIEC); those which experienced modest growth (other Baptist churches and the FIEC); and those which experienced rapid growth from a standing start in 1970 (the New Churches; other non-denominational churches; and the African and West Indian churches—ie, those within the charismatic and pentecostal streams). The Christian Brethren stand out by their consistent rapid rate of decline since 1970.

The insistent question is therefore, why are other Evangelical groupings growing or at least not declining while the Christian Brethren are? Elsewhere in this volume, it is suggested that Brethren churches face a further 10% decline in the 1990s simply as a result of the age structure of their membership. It is clear that they have to find an answer to the insistent question—quickly! In this connexion, the evidence of the English Church Census is that it has not been essential to be 'charismatic' to experience church growth in recent years, but it is inescapable that the most rapidly-growing groups have shared such an approach to church life.

Table 20 gives details of the average size of congregation by denomination in the period 1970–1990. This issue is of interest because of the evidence from the English Church Census and earlier in this volume that congregational size has been relevant to prospects of growth in the last few years.

Overall across the denominations, Table 20 suggests a gentle decline in the average size of congregation which, given the method of computation, results from the fact that, as shown by Tables 18 and 19, in most denominations the number of church buildings/congregations has not been reduced sufficiently to match the overall reduction in membership in many cases. Exceptionally, this does not

Table 20: Average congregational size in the UK, 1970–1990

	1970	1975	1980	1985	1987	1990	1990 as % of 1970	1990 as % of 1980
Anglican	125	114	111	105	103	101	81	91
Roman Catholic	533	616	566	486	469	437	82	77
Methodist	69	67	65	68	65	64	93	98
Presbyterian	272	258	247	245	239	235	86	95
Baptist	80	75	71	72	70	70	88	99
of which Baptist Union	87	81	78	78	77	75	86	96
Other Baptist	42	37	39	48	44	48	114	123
Reformed churches	92	79	74	76	76	81	88	109
of which FIEC	53	48	49	69	70	78	147	159
House churches	100*	66	73	83	62	56	56	77
Pentecostal/Holiness	81	71	73	64	73	74	91	101
Afro-Caribbean	56	68	77	74	72	72	129	94
Salvation Army	86	93	78	59	59	67	78	86
Christian Brethren†	42	40	39	42	41	41	98	105
All other denominations	193	191	190	165	226	204	106	107
TOTAL	164	157	151	140	138	133	81	88

Notes: * 1 congregation only; † UK Christian Handbook figures.

seem to have happened in the case of the Christian Brethren whose average congregational size has remained fairly constant over the last two decades. The estimated number of congregations seems to have fallen broadly in line with the fall in overall membership. This may result from the absence of any infrastructure to keep open and maintain buildings where there is insufficient resource from within the particular congregation itself. Declining numbers may result more from the demise of congregations than from reduction in the size of existing congregations (though this deduction is somewhat at odds with the perception of the majority of respondents to the 1988 survey that their congregational number had been reduced in the preceding two years).

Table 20 also suggests a significant variation in the average congregational size between denominations. It is of interest that of those included in the Table the Christian Brethren have the smallest average congregational size. Only the 'Other Baptists' (in fact largely the Strict Baptists) have a comparable average congregational size. The much larger congregational size in the older established denominations may in part reflect differing perceptions of the nature and purposes of congregational life and the commitment which it should imply. The significant increase in average congregational size in FIEC churches during the past two decades (by nearly 50%) is noteworthy, as is the expansion of their ministerial cadre more than to match (see Table 21). It is also of interest that the average size of New and House Church congregations may be more than double the average size of Brethren congregations. Quite apart from spiritual attitudes, there could be some relationship between congregational size and the differing growth experiences of the two groupings.

Figures for the numbers in full-time ministry (by which is meant, in most denominations, ordained officials) are of particular interest because of the strong movement in many Christian Brethren congregations in the last 15 years to introduce a full-time congregational ministry, in many places motivated by a desire to reverse congregational decline. Such figures also open up the possibility of attempt-

Table 21: Full-time workers (i.e. ordained ministers) in UK churches, 1970–1990

	1970	1975	1980	1985	1987	1990	1990 as % of 1970	1990 as % of 1980
Anglican:								
Number	17,379	15,911	14,654	14,061	13,790	14,072	81	96
No./Congn.	0.85	0.80	0.76	0.74	0.74	0.77		
Members/Min.	146	142	147	141	140	131		
R. Catholic:								
Number	8,130	8,001	7,642	8,456	7,896	7,630	94	100
No./Congn.	1.59	1.94	1.84	1.94	1.80	1.71		
Members/Min.	334	317	306	251	261	255		
Methodist:								
Number	2,789	2,610	2,421	2,382	2,349	2,336	84	96
No./Congn.	0.28	0.29	0.28	0.30	0.30	0.31		
Members/Min.	249	236	224	212	220	207		
Presbyterian:								
Number	4,153	3,842	3,715	3,404	3,290	3,107	75	84
No./Congn.	0.63	0.60	0.61	0.60	0.58	0.56		
Members/Min.	435	428	406	407	409	416		
Baptist:								
Number	2,483	2,362	2,421	2,648	2,722	2,906	117	120
No./Congn.	0.67	0.65	0.72	0.78	0.79	0.85		
Members/Min.	119	114	99	92	89	83		

Table 21 continued

Afro-Caribbean:								
Number	1,517	870	1,032	1,437	1,586	2,001	132	194
No./Congn.	2.64	1.25	1.22	1.60	1.72	2.07		
Members/Min.	21	54	63	46	42	35		
Salvation Army:								
Number	1,647	1,511	1,451	1,613	1,610	1,692	103	117
No./Congn.	1.55	1.51	1.52	1.60	1.69	1.83		
Members'Min.	56	61	51	37	35	37		
Christian Brethren:								
Number	100	150	150	144	143	140	140	93
No./Congn.	0.05	0.08	0.08	0.09	0.09	0.09		
Members/Min.	800	487	453	458	442	451		
All others								
Number	460	492	513	700	754	775	168	151
No./Congn.	0.33	0.34	0.35	0.38	0.45	0.40		
Members/Min.	580	557	548	437	501	509		
TOTAL								
Number	40,492	37,469	36,391	37,975	37,813	39,196	97	108
No./Congn.	0.76	0.73	0.73	0.76	0.75	0.77		
Members/Min.	217	215	207	186	183	173		

Notes: All figures calculated from data in *UK Christian Handbook 89/90* and *92/93 Editions.*

Table 21 continued

of which:								
B. Unions								
Number	2,024	1,890	1,825	1,952	2,009	2,143	106	117
No./Congn.	0.64	0.62	0.66	0.71	0.72	0.77		
Members/Min.	134	132	118	110	106	98		
Other Baptists								
Number	459	472	596	696	713	763	166	128
No./Congn.	0.84	0.83	1.02	1.12	1.12	1.17		
Members/Min.	51	44	38	43	39	41		
Reformed:								
Number	1,022	880	1,223	1,185	1,178	1,165	114	95
No./Congn.	0.59	0.48	0.64	0.66	0.67	0.69		
Members/Min.	157	200	113	114	113	119		
of which, FIEC:								
Number	290	306	607	630	640	654	226	108
No./Congn.	0.74	0.74	1.37	1.44	1.48	1.55		
Members/Min.	72	65	36	48	47	50		
House churches;								
Number	0	10	200	745	1,250	2,000	–	1000
No./Congn.	–	0.05	0.59	0.65	0.60	0.59		
Members/Min.	–	125	125	128	104	85		
Pentecostal/Holiness:								
Number	812	830	969	1,200	1,245	1,372	169	142
No./Congn.	0.71	0.70	0.80	0.96	0.99	1.07		
Members/Min.	113	101	92	66	74	70		

ing to discern some systematic relationship between numbers in full-time congregational ministry and the numerical fortunes of the congregations concerned. Table 21 suggests an indeterminate pattern, however, though there are some interesting features.

On the one hand, over the period since 1970 there has been a decline in numbers in the full-time ministry in the older, larger denominations, including the Baptist Union (though in that case the position stabilised in the 1980s) and in the older reformed groupings. The decline broadly parallels the decline in overall church membership. On the other hand, there has been a sharp increase in numbers in the full-time ministry in the more exclusively evangelical groupings—the Other Baptists, the FIEC, the House churches and the other non-denominational churches, the Pentecostal/Holiness churches, the African/West Indian churches, and the Brethren. These groups show however differing growths in membership and it is too early to say whether there is any close relationship between numbers in full-time ministry and church growth. Indeed, the numbers coming forward for congregational ministry at any time may well reflect spiritual fervour at that time of the denominational membership as a whole and their commitment to supporting local congregational life.

It is noteworthy that in few denominations over the last 20 years have numbers in full-time ministry approached one per congregation (which might be considered the norm traditionally). Generally, the proportion has been of the order of 0.6–0.7. Exceptions are the Roman Catholics, which have fewer and larger congregations; and the Other Baptists and FIEC in the 1980s. The African/West Indian churches and the Salvation Army are also widely out of line, in the former case because many ministers are also in secular employment, permitting more per congregation (an arrangement in principle like that of Brethren eldership). In the case of the Salvation Army, it may reflect the principle of ordaining husbands and wives jointly to congregational responsibility.

Generally, interpretation of the figures in Table 21 must be cautious because of the wide denominational differences in concepts of ministry in the church, and the suspicion that much full-time congregational ministry (eg, of women in secular and religious orders in the Roman Catholic church) is not included in the usual data on full-time ministers in the denominations concerned. Certainly, the figure of 165 for those in full-time congregational ministry in the Christian Brethren in 1990 is worth closer investigation and may be an under-estimate. If that is so, the growth in numbers in full-time ministry and the growth in membership in some evangelical groupings over the last two decades may perhaps be taken as an encouraging sign for Christian Brethren churches.

10

What Does All This Say?

The 1988 Survey of Brethren Churches may be summarised as follows:

1) A typical Brethren assembly had around 50 members in 1988. However the size of assemblies ranged from under 10 members to 300 plus members, with the average of 52 unchanged from 1978.

2) Between 1986 and 1988, 1 in 3 assemblies reported church growth but 4 in 9 assemblies experienced decline.

3) Between 1986 and 1988 the Brethren movement experienced a small net growth in numbers of 2.6%. However, the smallest assemblies as a group saw decline and the future viability of many in this group is in doubt.

4) Since 1978 the Gospel Meeting has seen a decline in its importance across the Brethren movement as a whole, while the Family Service and Prayer Meeting became increasingly more important.

5) A large majority of assemblies have systematic teaching, and a majority of assemblies use prearranged speakers for some of their teaching meetings. A majority of assemblies will also use outside speakers from time to time and some of these will be non-Brethren speakers.

6) Between 1986 and 1988, 1 in 5 assemblies gained 10 or

more converts; however, 3 in 10 assemblies saw no conversions during this period. Only 1 in 2 of the smallest assemblies gained converts compared to 6 in 7 of the largest assemblies.

7) The traditional Gospel Meeting still has an important part to play as a method of evangelism but increasingly other evangelistic methods are also being used, particularly those that involve the church going out into the community such as door-to-door visitation and open air work.

8) Most Brethren assemblies have an eldership or oversight as their form of church government. More and more assemblies are introducing deacons as part of their leadership structure. Most Leadership teams meet on a monthly basis.

9) In a majority of Brethren assemblies new elders, deacons, etc, were solely appointed by members of the current Leadership team. An increasing number of assemblies are appointing full-time or part-time resident workers.

10) Where they were allowed in leadership, women usually served on a church committee.

11) Three-quarters of Brethren assemblies hold regular activities to encourage missionary interest and almost half commended and supported long- or short term missionaries.

12) Most assemblies had links with other assemblies and a majority had links with other evangelical churches.

The English Church Census findings reflect the independence of Open Brethren assemblies, and their mainstream evangelical standpoint. This helps the urban assemblies but hits the rural assemblies. A strong tradition of going twice on Sunday is apparent. But growth tends to be confined to the larger (and fewer) assemblies, and the age structure of those currently attending is likely to hinder much growth in the next decade as people are 'promoted to glory' as the Salvation Army put it.

The major concern must be the relative paucity of men of working age and men and women in their twenties. Traditionally, these groups have been among the main strengths of the Brethren, and the consequences of moving ahead without them are huge: they clearly represent the main motive force of any local church, providing, on the one hand, much of the congregational leadership, and, on the other, workers at the coal face of outreach and pastoral care. Urgent stategic action is needed in many churches to reach out in order to replace these strategic groups. In many congregations, it is one reason why full-time and part-time workers in these age-groups are needed in order to prime the pump of outreach to their peers.

Against the background of the fortunes of other denominations in the Seventies and Eighties, three lessons stand out in respect of the Brethren. First, the proportional decline of nearly one-fifth in total congregations since 1970 has been significantly greater than has occurred in any of the other Evangelical groupings with which the Brethren are broadly comparable. The decline has however not been so rapid as that of the largest 'mixed' denominations, which have typically experienced a decline in numbers of some 30% over the period. Secondly, Brethren congregations are on average among the smallest among the denominations. This may be of particular significance given that the evidence of the surveys of 1988 and 1989 is that growth is more likely to be found in churches which are considerably larger than the average—a point which is also reflected in the experience of other denominations. Thirdly, and much more tentatively, the growth of full-time congregational ministry in Brethren churches *could*, on the basis of some comparable denominations over the last 20 years, presage a return to growth in the churches concerned.

It has to be said that many of the general conclusions of the surveys are depressing and represent a major challenge to prayer and radical action to restore the fortunes of many congregations of Brethren origins. Clearly, there are signs of continuing spiritual life as evidenced for example by a limited number of conversions in recent years in many

congregations. Changes are being made in church pro-
grammes, teaching and leadership patterns in order to adapt
to the changing circumstances in which congregations find
themselves. There is a continuing missionary effort, often
taking new forms, which is substantial in relation to the size
of the denomination though on a smaller scale than in the
first 60 years of this century.

On the other hand, the sharp decline in numbers of
congregations, the static average membership of those that
remain, the small numbers of conversions of adults and
teenagers in recent years, the imminent departure of a
substantial number of elderly members do not augur well
for the immediate future. Though there may well have been
changes in some congregations since the survey of 1988, at
that date Brethren churches had in general drawn little on
developments in charismatic spirituality and practice which
have done so much to revive nonconformist Evangelicalism
over the past 25 years.

But above all, the survey data convey a marked sense
of tentativeness in the approach to change in many aspects
of church life, for example, to patterns of meetings and
outreach. Those who have been familiar with Brethren
congregations over the past few years would testify that in
many there is a new desire to experience blessing and
growth under the hand of God. The most fundamental
question posed by results recorded in this volume is however, whether there is a willingness to make changes which
are sufficiently radical to set the churches concerned on a
new path of growth in the last decade of the century.
Without that it is hard to see that the spiritual stirrings will
find practical expression in church growth.

Appendix 1:
Christian Brethren Growth, 1850–1960

Though quite a number of historical studies of the Christian Brethren in the British Isles have been published in the last thirty years, few statistics about them have been available. This appendix[1] attempts to bring together data on the growth of the denomination in terms of numbers of congregations and members, and to make some comparisons between the different countries and regions of the British Isles.[2]

The Christian Brethren congregations of the British Isles have their origins in the period of immense religious ferment following the second Evangelical awakening of 1805–1810. The first half of the nineteenth century was a time of enormous growth of Protestant Christianity in Great Britain, outstripping even the parallel dynamic growth of

---

1 Particular thanks are due to Peter Brierley, European Director of MARC Europe for his considerable help and encouragement in preparing these data; and to a number of others for kindly supplying copies of various editions of assembly address lists which have been one of the main sources.
2 It is sensible to regard the Christian (Open) Brethren as a denomination. Despite their lack of a centralised decision-making structure and the stalwart independency of the individual congregations, they have historically had a strong consistency of doctrine, practice, spiritual attitudes, and sense of common identity, though this homogeneity is now showing signs of breaking down.

the population as a whole. *Membership*[3] of Protestant churches grew from some 13% of the adult civil population in 1801 to a peak of 16.5% in 1851. And in that latter year *attendance* at morning service on a typical Sunday, as computed in Horace Mann's Census of Religious Worship, amounted to some 40%[3a] of the adult population of England and Wales. All Evangelical nonconformist groups shared in the growth in a broadly equivalent way.

It was a period of ferment too in terms of understanding of the nature and processes of the church. This was reflected in the emergence of new Methodist groups at odds with aspects of the Wesleyanism of that time (eg, the Bible Christians); the Tractarian movement in the Church of England; the Catholic Apostolic Church; and the Brethren movement.

In the last case, numbers of congregations and adherents remained small in the first two decades of the movement, before 1850. According to Mann's census of church attendance in 1851 there were 132 Brethren places of worship in England and Wales. Some no doubt belonged to the emerging Darbyite (Exclusive Brethren) wing of the movement. These buildings had 18,529 seats and were attended on census day by 5,699 people in the morning and 7,384 in the evening. (There were 4,509 attendances in the afternoon—at a guess mainly Sunday School children.)[4]

---

3 The distinction between membership and attendance is important. The latter refers to physical presence at religious worship. Membership of a congregation frequently requires a greater degree of commitment. For statistical purposes, it has perforce to be variously defined between denominations: for Anglicans, it is those on the electoral role of the parish; for Roman Catholics, it is those attending mass (and is therefore closer to 'attendance'); for Baptists, it is those admitted to formal membership by baptism or by acceptance by the congregation on personal testimony. On 'membership' of a Brethren congregation, see note 14 below. It is of course the case that while membership may imply greater commitment to the life of the particular congregation than attendance, attendance on any Sunday at a particular congregation may be smaller than the current membership of that congregation.

3a This is my computation from the figures given in the appendix to the work cited in the following note. Geoffrey Best cites a range of 47–54% (for attenders aged 10 years and over) in *Mid-Victorian Britain 1851–75*, London: Fontana/Collins, 1979, p. 197.

4 See tables in Robert Currie, Alan Gilbert and Lee Horsley, *Churches and churchgoers: patterns of church growth in the British Isles since 1700*, Oxford: Clarendon Press, 1977, p. 216.

The great period of growth of the Open Brethren assemblies took place in the second half of the nineteenth century and early in the twentieth century.[5] It resulted from the revivals of 1859–61; the evangelistic campaigning of Moody, Torrey and others; the work of Brethren evangelists such as John M'Vicker, Jeremiah Meneely, Joseph Denham Smith, Henry Moorhouse, James Turner, Russell Hurditch and many others;[6] and deep evangelistic zeal at the local level, which characterised the earlier generations of the movement and is still deeply embedded in the tradition today. It was a numerical advance which was shared by the Primitive Methodists in rural areas in the third quarter of the nineteenth century, and by the Salvation Army in the forty years after 1880. It failed however to avert the deceleration in church growth which resulted from the fading performance of the older nonconformist denominations in these years.[7]

The growth and strength of the Christian Brethren as a denomination over the years since 1880 can be shown by the number of congregations included in the lists of assembly addresses which were published periodically.[8] The limitations of these lists for statistical purposes are real—they cannot be regarded as complete and their explicit purpose was to help holidaymakers, travellers, and those moving to new areas to 'find a Company of christians cleaving to God and to "the Word of His grace" (Acts 20:32), and where one (1) truly "born again", (2) sound in faith, and (3) godly in

---

5 Much Brethren history has focussed on the first 20 years of the movement, but understandably at that stage numbers were small.

6 See F Roy Coad, *A history of the Brethren movement*, Exeter: The Paternoster Press, second edition, 1976, pp. 165–186; Neil Dickson, 'Scottish Brethren: division and wholeness, 1838–1916', in *Scottish Brethren 1838–1916 and other papers, Christian Brethren Review*, No. 41 (ed. Harold Rowdon), Exeter: The Paternoster Press, 1990, pp. 5–41.

7 See A D Gilbert, *Religion and society in industrial England: church, chapel and social change, 1740–1914*, London: Longman, 1976, pp. 42–44.

8 The first of these lists of which I am aware was published in April 1886 by Sprague and revised the following January. Further lists were published in September 1897 and 1904 by J W Jordan. Pickering and Inglis of Glasgow published lists in 1922, 1933, 1951, 1959, 1970, 1975 and 1983. In 1990 and 1991 the task was taken up by Christian Year Publications of Bath.

life will be "received to the glory of God" (Rom. 15:7)."[9] Occasionally the address of a congregation already defunct may have been included. But apart from that the lists can reasonably be taken as indicating the *minimum* number of Open Brethren congregations in the British Isles when each list was published.

Tables 1–3 give the numbers of congregations based on these lists. In general, they bear out the more conservative contemporary estimates in the Brethren journals.[10] They verify the very rapid growth between 1850 and the early years of the twentieth century—a four and a half fold increase in England and Wales between 1851 and 1887 (counting all the 1851 congregations as Open Brethren), and a sixfold increase between 1851 and 1904. In Scotland and Ireland (mainly the province of Ulster) over the same period the establishment of new congregations was even more dramatic, as Table 1 shows.

In the following 50 years growth continued but much less rapidly as the denomination entered the familiar phase of maturity. The total increase in congregations was some 40% between 1904 and 1933. There was an apparent dip to 1951, followed by a return in 1959 to the level of 1933. In turn, that was followed by a 19% decline in the 32-year period to 1991.

The dip in the number of congregations in the decades around the Second World War is interesting—the assemblies were not exceptional in experiencing difficulties during the war years. But the pattern suggests too that in the 1950s

---

9 *List of Some Assemblies in the British Isles, where Believers professedly gather in the Name of the Lord Jesus for Worship and Breaking of Bread in Remembrance of Him upon the first Day of the Week*, London and Glasgow: Pickering and Inglis, [1922], Editor's Note.
10 Brethren journals gave a wide range of estimates in the first 40 years of the century. By 1912, 2,000 assemblies were estimated to have 60,000 members (*Links of Help*, April 1912, editorial). In 1937, F Broadhurst estimated that there were 1,600 assemblies in the British Isles (*Harvester*, December 1937, p. 276); in 1939, F A Tatford estimated that there were 'less than 2,000 assembly halls in the whole of the British Isles' (*Harvester*, April 1939, p. 73); and the *Echoes of Service Annual Report* said in 1940 that there were 'more than 1,600 gatherings in the British Isles' (*Harvester*, June 1940, p. 95). (Information provided by Dr H H Rowdon.)

new congregations were still coming into being, probably on the burgeoning estates around the main towns and cities.[11]

Table 2 indicates the broad and relatively even geographical spread of Brethren congregations. The proportionate shares of congregations by region have also been reasonably stable since 1900. There are however some noteworthy changes, such as the gradually declining proportion of congregations in Scotland; the expected strength in south-west England; and the comparatively thin numbers in the north-east and north-west. The increasing proportion in Wales is notable too. In fact, the churches were located mostly in English-speaking south Wales and the coastal strip in north Wales which in this century has increasingly been peopled by migrants from north-west England and the Midlands. There have, it appears, been virtually no assemblies in predominantly Welsh-speaking areas.

The relative strength in the south-west compared with the north of England is borne out by the data in Table 4. In the first half of the twentieth century, there were, proportionate to population, 10 times as many assemblies in the south-west as in the north-east, and 6 times as many as in the north-west.

There are other suspicions too from the address lists: that assemblies were strongly represented in rural areas in the south, south-west and East Anglia in the nineteenth century; but that growth in numbers of congregations in the first 60 years of the twentieth century has been largely an urban and suburban phenomenon. This may reflect general patterns of migration,[12] as do the figures in Table 3, which suggest that decline since the 1950s in the cities has proceeded in parallel with the general decline of city population over the period: in the 10 cities listed a quarter (45) of

---

11 This dip takes the information in the address lists at face value. It is possible that the hiatus of war affected the address list more than the number of assemblies on the ground! For details of the impact of the world wars on church membership, see Robert Currie *et al.*, *op. cit.*, pp. 29–33.
12 In *Class and Religion in the late Victorian city* (London: Croom Helm , 1974), Hugh Macleod shows how the churches of Bethnal Green in the period 1880–1914 were fed by young migrants who had been converted in churches in rural areas.

Brethren congregations have gone out of existence in only 32 years.

Some data are available[13] which permit a comparison between the overall number of Brethren congregations and the total number of Christian congregations *in Great Britain* in the present century.

Year	No. of Protestant congregations	No. of RC congregations	No. of Brethren congregations	Brethren as % of Protestant congregations (inc. Brethren)
1906	33,907	2,021	1,071*	3.1%
1921	34,480	2,377	1,212*	3.4%
1933	34,328	2,755	1,555	4.5%
1951	33,645	3,419	1,394	4.0%

*Estimates based on the figures in Table 1

Open Brethren congregations have therefore in this century accounted for a minor, but up to 1970 growing, proportion of Protestant congregations in Great Britain.

Information on total membership[14] of Brethren congregations is much more limited. The average morning attendance at the 132 meetings recorded by Mann in 1851 was approximately 43—there might have been some absent believers, and on the other hand it is possible that some attenders could not have been regarded as committed members. Half a century later, a detailed census of church attendance in the London area was undertaken under the auspices of *The Daily Mail*: average morning attendance by adults at the 81 congregations which can positively be

13 The numbers for non-Brethren congregations are those (with some interpolation) given by Peter Brierley in Table 13.3 of his article 'Religion' in *British Social Trends since 1900: A Guide to the Changing Social Structure of Britain*, ed. A H Halsey, London: Macmillan, second (revised) edition, 1988, p. 526.
14 Many Brethren congregations do not keep membership lists and have no formal concept of membership: 'informally recognised long-term adherence to the congregation' would be the closest to 'membership' in the form practised by some other nonconformist denominations. However informal, this status would only be given to those thought to be believers and not known to be tolerating serious sin in their lives—see note 3 above and the related text.

identified as Open Brethren was 43.6; in addition, 14.8 children were present on average.[15] Otherwise, there is no definite information on congregational size in the period up to 1960—though it is interesting that the figures in 1904 in London are not far different from those suggested by more recent surveys of the country as a whole (see pages 9–12 above).

However, assuming the averages were alternatively 40, 60 and 80, the following are the possible ranges of total membership since the 1880s in the British Isles:–

Year	Assumed average size of congregation		
	40 adults	50 adults	80 adults
1887	33,520	50,280	67,040
1904	49,440	74,160	98,880
1922	57,600	86,400	115,200
1933	69,560	104,340	139,120
1951	63,080	94,620	126,160
1959	69,440	104,160	138,880

The probability is that the average membership of Brethren churches over this period was always towards the lower end of this range. If so, that tends to bear out a 1912 estimate of 60,000 members and Roy Coad's estimate that there were between 75,000 and 100,000 members of Brethren congregations in the British Isles in 1959, when total membership was probably at its numerical peak.[16] This may be compared with the total membership of the major Protestant denominations in 1960 of 5.3 millions[17] *in the United Kingdom*, ie, the Brethren accounted for about 2% of total Protestant church membership, but 6% of nonconformist membership (ignoring Scottish Presbyterians as well as Anglicans in Scotland).

---

15 Data compiled from the tables in ed. Richard Mudie-Smith, *The religious life of London*, London: Hodder and Stoughton, 1904.
16 Roy Coad, *op. cit.*, p. 186.
17 *British Social Trends since 1900*, p. 154.

Table 1: Christian (Open) Brethren Congregations in the British Isles

	1851	1887‡	1897	1904	1922	1933	1951	1959	1970	1975	1983	1991
London		94†	97†	107†	99†	104†	70* (149†)	76* (161†)	148*	63*	52*	45*
England & Wales (excl. London)	132§	481	597	676	834	1,078	985	1,151	1,071	1,127	1,076	919
Scotland	2¶	184	236	288	331	373	339	324	296	299	274	251
Ireland	–	79	146	165	176	184	183	185	192	191	185	183
TOTAL		838	1,076	1,236	1,440	1,739	1,577	1,736	1,707	1,680	1,585	1,407

Notes

Sources: Periodic address lists of Assemblies – see note 8 above.

‡ *The Eleventh Hour*, January 1887, p. 4.

† Wider London area

* London postal area

§ Horace Mann's Census of Religious Worship 1851 (see tables in Robert Currie, Alan Gilbert, Lee Horsley, *Churches and Churchgoers: Patterns of Church Growth in the British Isles since 1700* (Oxford: Clarendon Press, 1977), p. 216). These figures may well include Exclusive Assemblies.

¶ Information from Neil Dickson (Kilmarnock).

Table 2: Christian (Open) Brethren Congregations in the UK†: Regional Distribution

	1896	1904	1922	1933	1951	1959	1970	1975	1983	1990	1991
UK Total	1,036	1,192	1,406	1,694	1,555	1,715	1,686	1,656	1,555	1,404	1,380
Scotland	236	288	331	373	339	324	296	299	274	265	251
	(23%)	(24%)	(23%)	(22%)	(22%)	(19%)	(18%)	(18%)	(18%)	(19%)	(18%)
Wales	32	33	42	78	85	93	100	105	107	94	93
	(3%)	(3%)	(3%)	(5%)	(5%)	(5%)	(6%)	(6%)	(7%)	(7%)	(7%)
N. Ireland	106	121	142	139	161	164	171	167	155	156	165
	(10%)	(10%)	(10%)	(8%)	(10%)	(10%)	(10%)	(10%)	(10%)	(11%)	(12%)
London	97	107	99	104	149	161	148	63	52	44	45
	(9%)	(9%)	(7%)	(6%)	(10%)	(9%)	(9%)	(4%)	(3%)	(3%)	(3%)
South-West‡	133	154	160	194	169	147	178	183	165	176	170
	(13%)	(13%)	(11%)	(11%)	(11%)	(9%)	(10%)	(11%)	(11%)	(12%)	(12%)
North-East++	49	49	68	91	80	86	86	84	79	68	67
	(5%)	(4%)	(5%)	(5%)	(5%)	(5%)	(5%)	(5%)	(5%)	(5%)	(5%)
North-West¶	67	68	77	90	91	100	107	100	99	86	96
	(6%)	(6%)	(5%)	(5%)	(6%)	(6%)	(6%)	(6%)	(6%)	(6%)	(7%)
Rest of England	316	372	487	625	481	640	600	655	624	515	493
	(30%)	(31%)	(35%)	(57%)	(31%)	(37%)	(36%)	(40%)	(40%)	(37%)	(36%)

Notes:

†   England, Wales, Scotland and N. Ireland

*   See Table 1 for definitions

‡   The pre-1974 administrative counties of Cornwall, Devon, Dorset and Somerset, including county boroughs.

++   Northumberland, Co. Durham and Yorkshire, including county boroughs.

¶   Cumberland, Westmorland and Lancashire, including county boroughs.

Table 3: Christian (Open) Brethren Congregations in the UK: Selected Provincial Cities

	1896	1904	1922	1933	1951	1959	1970	1975	1983	1990	1991
Birmingham	12	15	21	24	32	35	36	35	31	20	21
Bradford	10	9	9	8	6	6	6	5	4	3	3
Bristol	9	9	14	19	18	24	25	26	22	19	21
Cardiff	10	9	8	23	19	21	20	19	21	17	19
Leeds	1	2	4	4	4	5	3	3	3	3	3
Liverpool	12	12	13	14	14	16	18	16	16	12	12
Manchester	12	14	13	14	15	18	19	15	15	16	14
Newcastle	2	2	2	1	4	4	4	4	4	4	4
Glasgow	25	33	34	36	32	32	22	20	16	18	17
Belfast	6	8	12	12	22	24	25	24	23	26	23

Table 4: Ratio of Brethren Churches to Total Population
(1 Congregation: '000 of population)

	1901	1921	1931	1951	1961
England					
and Wales	41.54	40.61	33.80	41.47	37.57
Scotland	15.53	14.75	12.98	15.03	15.95
South-West	10.50	10.73	9.07	11.74	14.14
North-East	117.81	94.29	73.77	75.65	82.13
North-West	69.17	68.48	59.64	60.11	55.53
Remainder					
of England					
and Wales					42.23
Birmingham	101.46	43.76	41.47	34.78	
Bradford	31.10	32.33	37.37	48.66	
Bristol	36.50	29.93	20.89	18.46	
Cardiff	18.22	27.50	9.74	12.84	
Liverpool	58.66	61.92	61.14	56.36	
Manchester					
Glasgow	27.80	30.41	30.22	34.06	
Belfast	43.62	34.58	36.50	20.18	

Population data from B R Mitchell and P Deane, *Abstract of British Historical Statistics*, 1962 and B R Mitchell and H G Jones, *Second Abstract of British Historical Statistics* (Cambridge University Press, 1971).

These figures put the Open Brethren into perspective
—though perhaps they do not do justice to their influence in
Evangelicalism through their prominence in para-church
bodies and through departures to other denominations in
the period since the Second World War. It is interesting that
in the past 25 years the growth of the New and House
Church movement in the United Kingdom has exceeded
anything that the Open Brethren ever experienced.[18]

---

18 See Table 19a in *UK Christian Handbook 1992/93* (p. 222) which estimated
congregations at 3,400 and membership at 190,000 in 1990.

Appendix 2:

Questionnaire for 1988 Survey of Brethren Assemblies

We are undertaking a study of assemblies which is looking into Brethren assemblies and their activities. This is a nationwide study and is a follow-up to a similar one which was carried out ten years ago in 1978. We shall be grateful for your cooperation in answering some questions for us. Your answers will be treated in the utmost confidence, and you can rest assured that nothing you say will be attributed to you or your assembly by name in any report of the findings without prior permission. The questions are designed to provide information about the background and make-up of assemblies and to help identify trends and the reasons behind their growth or decline in order to learn lessons that might help us all.

	DO NOT WRITE HERE
	REF NO

Name of Assembly...

Address...

....

Name and Address of Respondent...

....

	1
	2
	3
	4

Question

RING APPROPRIATE ANSWER

1.	What is the size of your assembly? About how many are in fellowship/membership? or how many Christians attend services regularly?	1-9	1	
		10-19	2	
		20-29	3	
		30-39	4	
		40-49	5	5
		50-59	6	
		60-69	7	
		70-79	8	
		80-89	9	
		90-99	0	
		100-109	1	
		110-119	2	
		120-129	3	
		130-139	4	
		140-149	5	
		150-199	6	6
		200-249	7	
		250-299	8	
		300+	9	
2.	Has the total number in Q1 increased or decreased over the past five years? Greatly or slightly?	Greatly increased (30% OR MORE)	1	
		Slightly increased (0 - 29%)	2	
		No change	3	
		Slightly decreased (0 - 29%)	4	7
		Greatly decreased (30% OR SO)	5	
3.	Thinking back to 1978 is the assembly bigger/smaller/ about the same in numbers as in 1978?	Bigger in number	1	
		About the same	2	
		Smaller in number	3	8
		Don't know	4	

95

			DO NOT WRITE HERE

4. In the last two years how many new   Write in
    people have come into fellowship?   number.......................   9
                                                                                       10

5. Into which of the following categories would   Write in
    these new members fit?   number

    Transfer from another church in the locality 11/12

    Transfer from another church some distance away 13/14

    Child of current church members 15/16

    Convert joining as full member(aged under 20) 17/18

    Adult convert joining as full member 19/20

6. In the last two years how many
    people have left the fellowship   . Write in number...........................   21/22
    (for whatever reason)?

7. Into which of the following categories would   Write in
    these fit?   number

    Transferred to another church in the locality 23/24

    Transferred to another church some distance away 25/26

    Died 27/28

    Stopped attending for other reason 29/30

8. What is the % in each age group   0-20 years ——   31/32
    in the assembly?   20-40 years ——   33/34
                                                 41-60 years ——   35/36
                                                 61+ years ——   37/38
                                                 Don't know ——   39/40

9. Do most members live within walking   Yes   1
    distance of the assembly?   No   2   41

10. Church Activities -Turn to separate Blue Sheet.

The Bible Teaching Programme

11. Do you have a systematic programme   Yes   1
    for your Bible teaching?   No   2   42

    IF 'YES' ANSWERED IN Q11 GO TO Q12, IF NO GO TO Q13

12. Which services or activities do you consider
    form part of this systematic programme?   TICK IF APPLIES

    Bible Teaching meeting   1
    Family Service   2   43
    Ministry following Breaking of Bread   3
    Other Sunday Service   4
    House Group   5
    Other (write in)..   6

13. In an average year out of 50 main teaching meetings
    how many would.........   Write in   DO NOT
                                                               number   WRITE HERE

    have prearranged speakers 44/45
    have outside speakers 46/47
    have non-Brethren speakers 48/49
    be conversational Bible Studies 50/51
    be addressed by an itinerant full-time worker 52/53
    be taken by your own resident full-time worker 54/55
    Other arrangement (write in)........................... .... 56/57

14. Which of the following apply to your assembly?   Yes   No

    Is it getting increasingly difficult to get outside
    speakers for ministry meetings?   □   □

    Does the church have a structured programme for   1
    training young people who show promise in   □   □   2
    speaking or ministering the Word.   3

    Do women teach the church in main church
    meetings from time to time   □   □

Evangelism

15. How many conversions have taken place through the   Write in number
    evangelistic activities of the assembly in the
    past two years? 59/60

16. How many were adults (age 20+) ? 61/62

17. How many were children or young people? 63/64

18. How many people have been baptised in the
    past two years? 65/66

19. a) Which of the following methods of evangelism does
       your assembly utilise?   Yes   No   Importance
                                                             Rating
                                                             (seeQ 19b)

       Traditional Gospel Meeting   □   □   □   68
       Sunday Morning Family Service   □   □   □   69
       Package of youth activities catering from cradle to adulthood □ □ □ 70
       Adult evangelism through activities such as
          Wives' Meetings and Men's Groups   □   □   □   71
       Friendship Evangelism (concentration on
          developing friendships with workmates and/or
          neighbours with a view to positive witness) □ □ □   72
       Community activities such as Mums and Toddler Groups □ □ □   73
       Community activities which take place outside the building □ □ □ 74
       Open Air work   □   □   □   75
       Door to door visitation   □   □   □   76
       Small group evangelistic bible studies   □   □   □   77
       Calendar events/Guest Services(e.g.Mothers Day) □ □ □   78
       Other (write in)....................................... □ □ □   79

    b) How important are these activities to the church?
       For each activity you use mark how important each is
       by using the following scale:-
                        Very Important   1
                        Quite Important   2
                        Not very Important   3

Leadership

20. What is the form of assembly leadership?   Elders/Oversight   1
    (Tick more than one if applicable)   Deacons   2   1
                                                Brothers Meeting   3
                                                Committees (like Deacons) 4
                                                Other.................... 5

IF 'ELDERS', 'DEACONS' OR 'OVERSIGHT' TICKED GO TO Q21, IF NOT GO TO Q 26

21. How often does the leadership group meet?   Weekly   1
                                                Fortnightly 2   2
                                                Monthly   3
                                                Less often   4

22. Do you have <u>women</u> who serve in the following capacities?

	Yes	No		
Elders			1	3
Deacons			2	
On Church Committees			3	

23. Does the leadership group ever meet for special   Yes   1
    retreats, or weekends or something similar?   No   2   4

24a. Does the group meet with elders/leaders from   Yes   1
     other assemblies on a local or area basis?   No   2   5

                IF YES GO TO Q 24b) IF NO TO Q 25

24b. How often?   Monthly   1
                                                        Quarterly   2
                                                        Twice yearly 3   6
                                                        Annually   4
                                                        Other   5

25. How are the assembly elders/leaders chosen?   1
    By the current group   2
    By the current group in consultatation with the church   3   7
    By elections by the church   4
    Other (write in)..   5

    ....

26. Does the assembly have: Yes   No

    a vision statement   1
    a set of written objectives   2   8

27. Does the assembly have full or part/time resident workers?   Yes, full time   1
                                                                  Yes, part time   2   9
                                                                  No   3

28. Is there a likelihood that you will appoint one or more full   Yes   1   10
    or part time resident workers in the next two years?   No   2

    IF NONE ANSWERED TO Q27, GO TO Q30

29. FOR EACH FULL OR PART TIME RESIDENT WORKER
    a)What are his/her chief responsibilities?
    b) Howis he/she remunerated?

    1st worker(M/F)...   11

      12

      13

DO NOT
WRITE HERE

2nd worker.(M/F)..   14

....   15

....   16

3rd worker.(M/F)..   17

....   18

....   19

4th worker(M/F)..   20

....   21

....   22

Missionary Activities   23

30. Do you have regular missionary activities in your assembly?   Yes   1
                                                                   No   2

    IF YES GO TO Q 31, IF NO GO TO Q 32

31. What form do these take?   TICK IF APPLIES

    Regular missionary meetings for the whole church   1
    Missionary topics included in other meetings   2   24
    Regular missionary prayer meetings   3
    Missionary Sewing Meetings   4
    Missionary Study Class   5
    Other.......................................   6   25

32. Do you have any Missionaries commended from   Yes   1
    your assembly- both at home and overseas?   No   2

    IF 'YES' COMPLETE SECTION ON REAR OF BLUE SHEET   26

33. Do you have any short termhome or overseas   Yes   1
    missionaries commended from the assembly?   No   2

    IF YES FILL IN ON BLUE SHEET

Miscellaneous

34a. Does the assembly have links with:-   TICK IF APPLIES

    Other brethren assemblies   1   27
    Other local evangelical churches   2
    A local Council of Churches   3
    The Evangelical Alliance   4
    The British Council of Churches   5
    Other......................................   6

35. In the meetings of the church do any
    of the following activities take place?   28

    Tongue speaking (with interpretation)   1
    Prophecy   2
    Healing   3

Thank you for your assistance.

Q10a. What are the Main Services and Activities?
10b. How often are they held?
10c. What day are they held on?
10d. What time of day are they held?

RING
IF YES
COL 29/30

Activities	Q10a Yes/No	Q10b Frequency	Q10c Day of week	Q10d Time of Day	Do not write here
Breaking of Bread	1	31	46		
Sunday School	2	32	47		
Gospel Meeting	3	33	48		
Family Service	4	34	49		
Bible Teaching/ Ministry Meeting	5	35	50		
Prayer Meeting	6	36	51		
Women's Meeting	7	37	52		
Teenage Bible Class/ Covenanter Group	8	38	53		
Young People's Fellowship (or similar)	9	39	54		
Secular Youth Club	0	40	55		
Wives Group (or similar)	X	41	56		
Mens' Group	V	42	57		
House Groups	1	43	58		
Mum's and Toddlers Group	2	44	60		
Other (write in)............	3	45	61		
....					
....					

For each Commended Worker please state
32a. Name
32b. Linked with Echoes of Service?
32c. With a Missionary Society? Which?
32d. Area of world?
32e. Field of Activity?
32f. Jointly Commended with another church?
32g. Short or long term?

Q32a	Q32b	Q32c	Q32d	Q32e	Q32f	Q33		
Name	Echoes link	Missionary Society	Area of world	Jointly Commended	Field of activity.	Short or long term	Do not write here	
							62	1234567890
							63	1234567890
							64	1234567890
							65	1234567890
							66	1234567890
							67	1234567890
							68	1234567890
							69	1234567890

Appendix 3:

Complete Data from the 1988 Survey

Question 1: What is the size of your assembly? About how many are in fellowship/membership? or how many Christians attend services regularly?

Column Number	Code Number		No	%		
5	1	1–9	12	4	Mean	52
	2	10–19	42	14	Average	
	3	20–29	55	18		
	4	30–39	34	11	Median	47
	5	40–49	32	10	Number	
	6	50–59	33	11		
	7	60–69	14	5	Modal Size	20–29
	8	70–79	21	7		
	9	80–89	20	7		
	0	90–99	16	5		
6	1	100–109	3	1		
	2	110–119	6	2		
	3	120–129	4	1		
	4	130–139	7	2		
	5	140–149	2	1		
	6	150–199	3	1		
	7	200–249	0	0		
	8	250–299	0	0		
	9	300+	1	0		
	0		305	100		

Question 2: Has the total number in Q1 increased or decreased over the past 5 years? Greatly or slightly

			No	%
7	1	Greatly increased	32	10
	2	Slightly increased	88	29
	3	No change	49	16
	4	Slightly decreased	111	36
	5	Greatly decreased	25	8
		Don't know	0	0

Question 3: Thinking back to 1978, is the assembly bigger/smaller about the same number as in 1978

			No	%
8	1	Bigger in number	101	33
	2	About the same	71	23
	3	Smaller in number	131	43
	4	Don't know	2	1

Questions 4–7: *In the past two years how many people have come into/left the fellowship?*

Transferring in

	All	Largest 100 Churches	Smallest 100 Churches	All	Largest 100 Churches	Smallest 100 Churches
	Average Number	*Average Number*	*Average Number*	*%*	*%*	*%*
Total Increase	8.6	17.5	3.8	18	20	21
Local Transfer	1.7	2.7	1.1	4	3	6
Distant Transfer	2.8	5.4	1.6	6	6	9
Child of Members	1.1	2.2	0.5	2	3	3
Youth joining	1.3	3.3	0.1	3	4	1
Adult joining	1.7	3.8	0.4	4	4	2

Transferring out

	All	Largest 100 Churches	Smallest 100 Churches	All	Largest 100 Churches	Smallest 100 Churches
	Average Number	*Average Number*	*Average Number*	*%*	*%*	*%*
Total Decrease	7.4	12.8	4.4	16	15	25
Local Transfer	2.1	3.4	1.7	4	4	9
Distant Transfer	2.9	5.0	1.4	6	6	8
Died	1.6	2.5	1.0	3	3	5
Other	1	2.1	0.4	2	2	2

Net Gains/Loss

	All	Largest 100 Churches	Smallest 100 Churches	All	Largest 100 Churches	Smallest 100 Churches
	Average Number	*Average Number*	*Average Number*	*%*	*%*	*%*
Total Gain/Loss	1.2	4.7	–0.6	3	5	–3
Transfer Growth	–0.5	–0.2	–0.4	–1	0	–2
Biological Growth	–0.5	–0.4	–0.5	–1	0	–3
Conversion Growth	2.0	5.0	0.2	4	6	1

Notes: Figures given are averages for the category
Percentages are based on the average (median) size church in the category
Source: 1988 Survey of GB Brethren Churches

Question 10: Activities—All Churches, Large, Small and Comparison with 1978

	All	Largest 100 Churches	Smallest 100 Churches
Base No	295	100	100
	%	%	%
Breaking of Bread	100	100	100
Prayer Meeting	96	95	85
Bible Teaching	91	94	75
Sunday School	82	91	59
Women's Meeting	73	88	48
Young People's Fellowship	51	80	17
Family Service	64	72	40
Gospel Meeting	77	68	79
Bible Class	52	66	24
House Groups	32	48	14
Wives Group	29	43	10
Mums & Toddlers Group	25	41	6
Youth Club	24	40	7
Mens Group	7	14	1

	Number
Breaking of Bread	295
Prayer Meeting	283
Bible Teaching	269
Sunday School	242
Women's Meeting	216
Young People's Fellowship	150
Family Service	188
Gospel Meeting	226
Bible Class	153
House Groups	93
Wives Group	85
Mums & Toddlers Group	74
Youth Club	72
Mens Group	21
Don't Know/No Reply	10
Total	305

	1988 %	1978 %
Breaking of Bread	100	100
Gospel Meeting	77	93
Sunday School	82	91
Bible Teaching	91	87
Prayer Meeting	96	85
Women's Meeting	73	81
Young People's Fellowship	51	47
Family Service	64	43
Youth Club	24	37
Wives Group	29	28

Source: 1988 Survey of GB Brethren Churches

Question number	All Number	Largest 100 Churches Number	Smallest 100 Churches Number	All % 295
11 Have a systematic programme	205			69 Yes
				31 No
12 1 Bible Teaching				
2 Family Service				
3 Ministry following B of B				
4 Other Sunday Service				
5 House Group	Yes			Yes
14 1 Outside speakers are increasingly difficult to get	99			34
2 We have structured training for speakers	41			14
3 Women teach in main church meetings from time to time	13			4
	No			No
1 Outside speakers difficult to get	127			43
2 Structured Training for speakers	159			54
3 Women teaching	178			60

Source: 1988 Survey of GB Brethren Churches

Question 13: Teaching Meetings
In an average year out of 50 main teaching meetings how many would . . . .

	0 No	1-9 No	10 No	11-19 No	20 No	21-29 No	30 No	30-39 No	40 No	41-49 No	50 No	Don't Know No	Total No
Have Prearranged Speakers	41	14	6	8	9	12	9	18	15	23	139	11	305
Have outspoken speakers	50	33	28	28	16	38	18	26	28	20	8	12	305
have non-Brethren Speakers	132	99	27	19	7	7	0	0	0	0	0	14	305
be conversational Bible studies	154	29	13	24	14	12	7	7	11	3	21	10	305
be addressed by an itinerant full-time worker	107	136	28	17	4	2	1	0	0	0	0	10	305
Be addressed by your own resident fulltime worker	253	14	3	8	2	6	1	2	2	4	0	10	305

	0 %	1-9 %	10 %	11-19 %	20 %	21-29 %	30 %	30-39 %	40 %	41-49 %	50 %	Don't Know %	Total %
Have Prearranged Speakers	13	5	2	3	3	4	3	6	5	8	46	4	100
Have outside speakers	16	11	9	9	5	12	6	9	9	7	3	4	100
have non-Brethren Speakers	43	32	9	6	2	2	0	0	0	0	0	5	100
be conversational Bible studies	50	10	4	8	5	4	2	2	4	1	7	3	100
be addressed by an itinerant full-time worker	35	45	9	6	1	1	0	0	0	1	0	3	100
Be addressed by your own resident fulltime worker	83	5	1	3	1	2	0	1	1	1	0	3	100

	Average Number No	%
Have Prearranged Speakers	35	69
Have outside speakers	20	41
have non-Brethren Speakers	5	9
be conversational Bible studies	11	22
be addressed by an itinerant full-time worker	5	9
Be addressed by your own resident fulltime worker	3	5

Source: 1988 Survey of Brethren Churches

	All	Largest 100 Churches	Smallest 100 Churches	All	Largest 100 Churches	Smallest 100 Churches	
Questions 15/18: Numbers of Conversions Baptisms—Total and Adult—in past two years							
	Number	Number	Number	%	%	%	
Base	303	100	100	303	100	100	
0	89	14	51	29	14	51	i.e. 29% of churches had no conversions in the last two years
1–4	111	35	38	37	35	38	
5–9	44	20	4	15	20	4	
10+	59	31	7	19	31	7	
Adult Conversions in past two years							
0	135	32	61	45	32	61	
1–4	133	51	36	44	51	36	
5–9	22	10	2	7	10	2	
10+	11	7	1	4	7	1	
Child/Youth Conversions in past two years							
0	139	31	73	46	31	73	
1–4	94	38	15	31	38	15	
5–9	50	25	8	17	25	8	
10+	20	6	4	7	6	4	
Baptisms in past two years							
0	87	10	55	29	10	55	
1–4	127	35	41	42	35	41	
5–9	46	25	3	15	25	3	
10+	42	30	1	14	30	1	

Source: 1988 Survey of GB Brethren Churches

Evangelistic Methods

Question	Col No		All Number	Largest 100 Churches Number	Smallest 100 Churches Number	All %	Largest 100 Churches %	Smallest 100 Churches %
19	68	Traditional Gospel Meeting	222	64	83	73	64	83
	69	Family Service	156	65	34	51	65	34
	70	Youth Package	151	68	23	50	68	23
	71	Adult evangelism	156	63	36	51	63	36
	72	Friendship Evangelism	100	37	22	33	37	22
	73	Mums & Toddlers etc	89	42	10	29	42	10
	74	Other Community activities	44	16	11	14	16	11
	75	Open Air Work	65	27	10	21	27	10
	76	Door to door	203	72	57	67	72	57
	77	Small group bible studies	69	29	16	23	29	16
	78	Callendar/Guest Services	182	71	38	60	71	38
		In order of priority						
		Traditional Gospel Meeting	222	64	83	73	64	83
		Door to door	203	72	57	67	72	57
		Calendar/Guest Services	182	71	38	60	71	38
		Family Service	156	65	34	51	65	34
		Adult evangelism	156	63	36	51	63	36
		Youth Package	151	68	23	50	68	23
		Friendship Evangelism	100	37	22	33	37	22
		Mums & Toddlers etc	89	42	10	29	42	10
		Small group bible studies	69	29	16	23	29	16
		Open Air Work	65	27	10	21	27	10
		Other Community activities	44	16	11	14	16	11

Source: 1988 Survey of GB Brethren Churches

Leadership Questions

Question	Col No			All Number	Largest 100 Churches Number	Smallest 100 Churches Number	All %	Largest 100 Churches %	Smallest 100 Churches %
20	1	Type of	Elders/Oversight	280	97	79	93	97	79
	2	leadership	Deacons	102	50	15	34	50	15
	3	group	Brothers Meeting	20	0	13	7	0	13
	4		Committees	38	25	2	13	25	2
21	1	Frequency	Weekly	22	6	6	7	6	6
	2	of	Fortnightly	32	20	4	11	20	4
	3	leadership	Monthly	156	67	26	52	67	26
	4	meetings	Less Often	30	2	21	10	2	21
22	1	Women	Elders	3	0	2	1	0	2
	2	in	Deacons	39	19	4	13	19	4
	3	leadership	Church Committees	92	40	16	30	40	16
23	1	Special	Yes	56	38	5	19	38	5
	2	Retreats	No	34	19	8	11	19	8
24a	1	Local elders	Yes	57	23	14	19	23	14
	2	meetings	No	34	19	8	11	19	8
25	1	Selection	By current group	177	65	42	59	65	42
	2	of	Ditto with consultation	75	28	23	25	28	23
	3	elders	Elections in church	10	3	5	3	3	5
	4		Other	6	1	4	2	1	4
26	1	Objectives	Vision statement	47	25	7	16	25	7
	2		Written objectives	61	28	11	20	28	11
27	1	Fulltime	Fulltime	36	23	4	12	23	4
	2	Leaders	Part-time	23	6	8	8	6	8
28	1	Future possibility of fulltimer		45			15		

Source: 1988 GB Survey of Brethren Churches

Mission/miscellaneous Questions

Question	Col No	Do you have:	All Number	Largest 100 Churches Number	Smallest 100 Churches Number	All %	Largest 100 Churches %	Smallest 100 Churches %
30	1	Regular missionary activities	230	87	63	75	87	63
32	1	Commended missionaries	135	70	24	44	70	24
33	1	Short term	41	24	4	13	24	4
34a	1	Links Other assemblies	260	79	84	85	79	84
	2	with local evangelical churches	181	67	47	59	67	47
	3	local Council of Churches	54	25	11	18	25	11
	4	Evangelical Alliance	54	28	8	18	28	8
	5	British Council of Churches	1	1	0	0	1	0
		In the meetings of the church do any of the following activities take place:						
35	1	Tongues	12	4	2	4	4	2
	2	Prophecy	23	9	5	8	9	5
	3	Healing	20	7	3	7	7	3

Source: 1988 GB Survey of Brethren Churches

Appendix 4:

The Missionary Dimension of the Responding Churches

The questions in the survey questionnaire which related to missionary involvement beyond the confines of the local church were enumerated 32(a)–(g). 32(a) asked for the names of those who had been commended by the church for missionary work at home or abroad. 32(b) asked whether they were listed on the Daily Prayer Guide of *Echoes of Service*. 32(c) enquired whether they were connected with a missionary society, and, if so, which one. 32(d) called for information on the area of the world in which the missionaries were located. 32(e) asked if the missionary was commended jointly with another church. 32(f) enquired about their field of activity, eg, medical missions. 32(g) asked if the missionary was serving on a short-term or long-term basis.

On the whole, the questions were understood by the respondents, though some interpreted 'field of activity' in geographical rather than functional terms. 'Short-term' was not defined in the questionnaire, nor were respondents asked to specify the length of a short-term commitment —though some did.

The returns indicated that of the 308 churches that responded, 142 (not far short of 50%) had commended one or more people for full-time service in this country or abroad. The 308 churches had an aggregate membership of about 10,000. So, on average, every 25 church members had commended a full-time worker. In actual fact, the relationship of members to commended workers in churches with less than 40 members was about 10:1. This is the highest ratio of all denominations.

Of the total of 400 commended workers, 324 were serving abroad (this figure includes a few whose work was actually located in this country, but was in the service of societies whose field of operation was abroad). 153 of these 324 had a connection

111

with *Echoes of Service*; 146 were members of named missionary societies; 25 appeared to be totally independent. Of the 75 serving in the UK, 8 were linked with Counties Evangelistic Work, 38 with various societies, and 27 appeared to be totally independent. The majority (346 out of 400) had made a long-term commitment, though 1 in 8 were short-term workers. This proportion compares favourably with the 10% of all Protestant missionaries and the 11% of Roman Catholics listed in the 1989–90 *UK Christian Handbook* (p. 435) who were short-term workers.

As with all the statistics in this survey, it is hazardous to extrapolate. For example, it would be wildly inaccurate to deduce from the fact that the 308 responding churches sent out 153 missionaries linked with *Echoes of Service* that the 1,400 UK assemblies had sent out 695 missionaries linked with *Echoes*. For thanks to the meticulous care with which the number of missionaries linked with *Echoes* is recorded, we know that the total number in 1988 was in fact 333 (excluding the 48 overseas nationals married to spouses commended from the UK). That is, nearly half of the total of missionaries linked to *Echoes* were sent out by the 20% of Brethren churches which responded to Partnership's 1988 survey—this is a point at which we can see clearly that the response to the survey was not representative of the 1,400 Brethren assemblies as a whole in the UK. Similarly, the fact that the 308 churches have 146 missionaries with missionary societies does not mean that the 1,400 assemblies had sent out 684 with missionary societies. In this case, we do not have accurate information comparable to the *Echoes* statistics. But the researches of Barbara Baigent have shown that in 1988 the number of people commended from 'Brethren' churches for work overseas other than with *Echoes* was *at least* 276. Of these, 207 were serving abroad, long or short term, with missionary societies, 26 were working in the UK with societies whose field of operation was overseas, 40 were working abroad independently, and 3 were based in the UK but spend extended periods of time overseas.

We may conclude, therefore, that the number of 'Brethren' missionaries serving abroad in 1988 who were not listed in the *Echoes*' Daily Prayer Guide may have been almost as great as the number who were. This is perhaps the most remarkable point suggested by the section of the survey under discussion here, and one of the most remarkable features of the Brethren scene in the UK in 1988.